# CORVETTE
# GRAND SPORT

**Dave Friedman
& Lowell C. Paddok**
Foreword by Roger Penske

**MOTORBOOKS**
INTERNATIONAL

This edition published in 2004 by Motorbooks International, an imprint of MBI Publishing Company, Galtier Plaza, Suite 200, 380 Jackson Street, St. Paul, MN 55101-3885 USA

First published in 1989 by MBI Publishing Company

Motorbooks International titles are also available at discounts in bulk quantity for industrial or sales-promotional use. For details write to Special Sales Manager at Motorbooks International Wholesalers & Distributors, Galtier Plaza, Suite 200, 380 Jackson Street, St. Paul, MN 55101-3885 USA.

ISBN 0-7603-1926-X

**Front cover, top:** The Grand Sport 004 of Johnson Chevrolet, Dallas. Driven by Delmo Johnson and Dave Morgan at Sebring in 1964, the car suffered continuous mechanical woes, finally finishing 32nd overall. **Bottom:** Grand Sport 003 owned by Bob Paterson of Woodside, California. After being raced by Dick Doane, John Mecom, and Alan Sevadjian, and driven by Augie Pabst, Jim Hall and John Cannon, the car made its way to Paterson in 1973. It has been restored as of 1989 to its Sebring 1964 colors. *Maggie Logan*

**Frontis:** Jamey Mazzotta throws his restored Grand Sport 004 into a turn while vintage racing. *Maggie Logan*

**Title page:** The Jim Hall / Roger Penske Grand Sport 005 at Sebring, March 1964.

**On the contents page:** Zora Arkus-Duntov, the godfather of the Corvette and its lightweight racing derivative, the Grand Sport. *Maggie Logan*

**Back cover, left:** The Grand Sports' last gasp in the form of the two roadsters, 001 and 002, George Wintersteen raced 002, here at Watkins Glen in 1966, with moderate success in the USRRC series of 1966. **Right:** Sebring, March 1964. Into the night, the Mecom team 003 Grand Sport pits for a tire change.

Printed in Hong Kong

# Contents

# Acknowledgments

The accurate compilation of motorsports history is a bit like asking someone to recall the speech given by their high school valedictorian. Time dims memories, coloring them with impressions and emotions, greatly frustrating the remembrance of *what really happened*. Although the Grand Sport's era is just twenty-five years distant, many of its members have gone on to achieve exploits that overshadow the wins and losses of this orphaned sports car, making the telling of its story doubly difficult. Nonetheless, we have been greatly aided by many individuals who have graciously assisted us with their time and patience.

To begin, this project could never have gotten off the ground in the first place without the enthusiasm of Tim Parker, Barbara Harold and Michael Dregni of Motorbooks International. The encouragement and vision of these three people is appreciated.

Fortunately, most of the key players involved with the Grand Sports are still alive, and many volunteered their time to review both text and photographs. It is truly amazing how effectively photographs can stimulate memory, prompting wonderful stories and amusing anecdotes. Among those who have given of their time are Dick Guldstrand, Jim Hall, Delmo Johnson, Ed Lowther, John Mecom, Jr., Augie Pabst, Roger Penske, Alan Sevadjian, Dick Thompson and George Wintersteen.

Many individuals who worked with Chevrolet and who were involved with the Grand Sport also came to our aid. We are particularly indebted to Walt Zetye, the car's senior chassis designer, as well as Ashod Torosian and Gib Hufstader.

Enough cannot be said about the present and recent Grand Sport owners: Bob Paterson, Jamey Mazzotta, Jim Purvis and Ed Mueller have contributed prodigious quantities of photographs, records and time to this book.

We are particularly indebted to Bob Paterson, whose fifteen-year devotion to the Grand Sport marks him as one of the leading authorities on the subject. His willing and enthusiastic contributions proved to be invaluable.

Other people who made significant contributions were Norman Ahn and Dan Lugunbuhl of the Penske Corporation, Bill Preston of Gulf Oil, Mike Antonick, Larry Shinoda and Eric Gill. Jane Gossage and Peter Laun of Road America sent copies of records from Grand Sport races held there in the mid-sixties. Likewise, SCCA archivist Harry Handley helped fill in some gaps in the Grand Sport racing record. Tom Warth loaned books from his automotive emporium for research purposes. Nancy Bego transcribed the taped interviews. And automotive artist Bill Neale volunteered many of his terrific photos of Texan Grand Sports, including a Polaroid print that offered conclusive proof that Delmo Johnson's Grand Sport did indeed compete in La Carrera de Costa a Costa equipped with a cow catcher.

Most of the black and white photographs in this book were printed by the photographer at Professional Photo Images in Santa Barbara, California; those not printed by the photographer were done by Studio Photo Service in Hollywood, which also did all the print spotting and proof sheets. Color prints of the current cars were done by Janet Arzamendi of Carpenteria.

A special thanks goes to Maggie Logan, whose superb color photography is featured in the book. Maggie is one of the fine young talents on the photographic scene today; without her dedication and professionalism, this book would have been a difficult undertaking.

Finally, although both of us have made every effort to be fair to the Grand Sport's historical record, we are aware that new information will always await our discovery. We welcome with enthusiasm any discoveries or clarifications that will improve the story that we have presented.

Lowell C. Paddock, Los Angeles
Dave Friedman, Santa Barbara
May 1989

# Foreword by Roger Penske

It was in early 1963 that I first heard about the Corvette that Zora Arkus-Duntov called the "Lightweight." Of course, it wasn't my first experience with racing Corvettes. As a junior at Lehigh University, I took my Jaguar XK 120 down to Hauser Chevrolet in Bethlehem, Pennsylvania, and traded it in for a new red-and-white '57 roadster with all the competition equipment I could get, including a 4.56 rear axle and a fuel-injected 283. With that car I began my racing career. I took it to hillclimbs at Reading and Giant's Despair. Then came the moment of truth, my SCCA driver's test at Cumberland, Maryland, in the spring of '58. It was the solid-axle Corvette's heyday, and drivers like Dick Thompson and Fred Windridge were there. I passed my test, but my car didn't, losing its engine later in the day. To make matters worse, it came loose from the truck I was towing it with, went off the road and into a tree.

It would be awhile before I came back to Chevrolet and the Corvette. The individual responsible for that was Bill Mitchell, whom I'd met while racing my Porsche at Mosport. Mitchell invited me back to the GM Tech Center where I met engineers Frank Winchell and Zora Arkus-Duntov. Since I was working for Alcoa at the time, I volunteered to help Chevrolet cast some aluminum V–8 blocks, and that was the start of a long relationship.

Because of my racing experience, I was called on to help Chevrolet sort out the Grand Sport's chassis, which had really been designed to compete in production classes. Working at the Waterford race course, just outside Detroit, in the fall of 1963, we tested the new wider tires, wheels and other suspension modifications that would ultimately appear on the triumphant second-generation Grand Sports at Nassau later that year.

Nassau was always one of my favorite races, and I think my experience there gave me an edge when it came to the Grand Sports and Chaparrals. I had first raced there in 1960 in my Porsche RS60 and finished third. I moved up to second the following year in my Cooper, and won the GT race with John Mecom's Ferrari GTO in 1962. I did well with the Grand Sport in 1963, finishing third again. I have especially fond memories of the 1964 race, when I held off Ken Miles' monstrous Cobra prototype to win the GT race. The Cobra was usually the Corvette's nemesis, but not at Nassau. We didn't have the brakes that the Cobra had, but the Lightweight was very responsive. It was quicker than the Cobras—quicker than the Ferraris, too.

Speed was always the Grand Sports' strength, especially at Sebring. In 1964, its sheer horsepower allowed me to pass the Ferrari prototypes on the first lap. Of course, the Grand Sport was a front-engined car, and although it was plenty quick, it certainly wasn't a match for the mid-engined cars it was running against. We knew that at Sebring in 1966 with the Grand Sport roadster. It was a great car, but progress had passed it by. At the time it was all we had.

On the pages that follow, you will see and read about the scenes behind the scenes of the Grand Sports' successes and failures. Through the photographs, many of which have never been published before, you can share in what was a memorable era for me, one where racing was a less complicated sport. Back then, if your car broke down, you somehow found a way to keep it going, even if it meant borrowing a part off a production car—which was what we did when one of our halfshafts broke at Sebring.

The engineering experience derived from the Grand Sport and other racing Corvettes was crucial to developing Chevrolet's performance capability that later infused the Trans-Am Camaros, the NASCAR stockers and the Indy cars we race now. It was a great thrill for me to drive the Corvette Grand Sports, and certainly when you look at how far the levels of performance have evolved, those Grand Sports were as much a part of my racing success as today's Ilmor Indy Chevy V–8s.

Roger Penske
May 1989

# Chapter 1

# The Corvette goes racing

In the winter of 1962, General Motors was the mightiest industrial combine on earth. Together, its six automotive and truck divisions had the capacity to produce some 4.09 million vehicles. The Chevrolet Motor Division alone would sell 2.13 million cars that years, achieving a record market share of 31.5 percent.

Just seven years earlier, Chevrolet had astounded the automobile industry with its new, lightweight, high-compression small-block V–8. The performance promised by this technologically advanced powerplant caught the attention of one Carroll Shelby, a Texas sports car racer and dealer who believed that the marriage of a reliable American engine with a lightweight, responsive European chassis would create one heck of a good sports car. Shelby had originally approached GM on using one of its engines for his arranged marriage, but the Detroit colossus wanted nothing to do with it and sent Shelby packing. Shelby persisted, however, and his enthusiasm found a home at Ford, which agreed to give him a pair of *its* new V–8 engines to do with what he pleased.

General Motors would rue the day it turned away Carroll Shelby. In the winter of 1962, Chevrolet watched its all-new Corvette Sting Ray, the beneficiary of millions of engineering dollars, utterly humbled by an Anglo-American hybrid assembled by a few talented men in a Sante Fe Springs, California, speed shop.

## Godfather of the Corvette

One of those especially interested in this confrontation was Zora Arkus-Duntov, the impatient and pragmatic godfather of America's only production sports car. He had worked hard to make the Corvette as competitive on the racetrack as it was on the boulevard, and he was not about to let Shelby, Ford or AC put one over on his real McCoy.

Born in Belgium on Christmas Day 1909, Arkus-Duntov was educated in Leningrad, Russia, and Darmstadt, Germany, and emigrated to New York with his brother Yura and his wife Elfie in 1940. Two years later, Yura and Zora hung out their own engineering shingle, eventually developing the famous Ardun overhead-valve conversion for the Ford V–8. After witnessing the Corvette's New York debut at the Waldorf Astoria Hotel, Zora joined the Chevrolet engineering staff in 1953.

Soon after his enlistment, he began pushing for the replacement of the 1953–54 Corvette's original Blue Flame inline six with Chevrolet's new V–8. Once the V–8 joined the Corvette's option list in 1955, Chevy's sports car was off and running, establishing a two-way flying-mile record of 150.583 mph on the Daytona sand in January 1956.

Arkus-Duntov had shown that the Corvette could win, and he was not going to let the world forget about it. For 1956, Arkus-Duntov wanted to campaign the V–8 powered Corvette in Sports Car Club of America (SCCA) events. To do so, he needed a top-notch driver, and no one fit the bill better than Dr. Richard Thompson, a Washington, D.C., dentist who had made quite a name for himself in SCCA events at the wheel of a Jaguar XK 140. In the spring of 1956, Corvette driver and team organizer John Fitch contacted Thompson with an offer he couldn't refuse. "Fitch called wanting someone to race a Corvette in SCCA events," recalled Thompson, "but he wanted the car back after every race. All I had to pay was my plane transportation."

Thompson's first Corvette ride took place at Pebble Beach, California, that April. His mount performed admirably, jumping away from the pack and decisively assuming the lead on the first lap. But the Corvette's undoing would prove to be a nemesis that the car would not shake for years to come: "We led the race," lamented Thompson, "until the brakes fell apart." Nonetheless, Thompson finished the event first in class and wound up the season as C-Production champion. The results boded well for the 1957 season, when Chevrolet would unveil a fuel-injected version of its potent and reliable V–8.

As good as the Corvette and its V–8 were, those in the know at Chevrolet were well aware that something more sophisticated was needed to turn back the best that Europe had to offer in world-class endurance events such as Sebring and Le Mans. At Sebring in 1956, for example, the hurriedly prepared Corvette team could do no better than ninth overall. "Watching the race," wrote Karl Ludvigsen in *Star-Spangled Sports Car,* "it didn't take [Chevrolet General Manager] Ed Cole long to realize that no modified version of the stock Corvette would ever be able to challenge for the outright lead against the specialized sports-racing cars."

## Corvette racers

While Thompson was working his way through the 1956 season in the production Corvette, Arkus-Duntov had embarked on an ambitious project to build an exotic, ground-up prototype designed expressly for endurance racing. The Corvette SS, as this car would be known, blended a tubular space frame similar to that of the Mercedes 300SL with a substantially modified version of the forthcoming 1957 Corvette's 283 ci V–8. As 1957 was the first year for fuel injection on the production car, the SS was seen as the ideal vehicle to advertise its performance benefits. And thanks to some tuning on Arkus-Duntov's part, the output of the purpose-built SS motor was increased from 283 to 307 hp. Curiously, the body of the SS was made not of the typical Corvette fiberglass but of a magnesium alloy.

The SS's maiden appearance was set for the Sebring twelve-hour race in March 1957. As race day approached, however, the SS was far from ready. While Chevrolet engineers in Detroit rushed to complete the car that would actually run at the race, testing at Sebring was consigned to a rough, barely bodied prototype known

Some of the most exciting racing of the early sixties occurred during the West Coast big-bore production races, which were hard-fought, fender-breaking affairs. The type of action shown here between two of the best, Paul Reinhart (6) and Dave MacDonald (00), was typical of these crowd-pleasing races. Note the black tape and missing headlight on the left fender of the Reinhart car. By mid–1962 these races had pretty much become all-Corvette affairs—and that called for a challenger.

as the Mule. During practice laps, drivers Juan Manuel Fangio and Stirling Moss both turned competitive times in the Mule, but without a finished car to drive, Chevrolet could lure neither driver to pilot the car in the race.

As time ran out, Chevrolet turned to racer John Fitch to oversee the Sebring effort. With virtually no development time available for testing of the completed car, the theory was to transfer the lessons learned from the Sebring Mule directly to the race car in Detroit. Reality was less rose-colored; with the SS arriving in Florida the day before the race, Fitch quickly realized the impossibility of updating the race car in the few hours that remained. "The Corvette SS had a lot of problems," Fitch later told historian Mike Antonick; "insurmountable problems." Lacking sufficient time to remedy those problems, the SS lasted just twenty-three laps, with co-driver Piero Taruffi eventually telling Ed Cole that the car would never finish the race.

In spite of the disappointing Sebring results, the SS had at least proven that a purpose-built racer had potential. Yet no sooner had plans been set for an assault on Le Mans than the Automobile Manufacturers Association (AMA) enacted a June 1957 ban on racing in hope of calming the nation's burgeoning horsepower war. The ban stated, in part, that auto makers "should encourage owners and drivers to evaluate passenger cars in terms of useful power and ability to provide safe, reliable and comfortable transportation, rather than in terms of capacity for speed." The effect on Chevrolet's racing efforts was immediate: the SS program was disbanded.

Nonetheless, racing went on, either on foreign soil or in the hands of privateers. In the winter of 1958–59, the SS Mule chassis was resuscitated by GM Design Vice President Bill Mitchell, the better for it to wear a stunning new body created by his styling department. Due to GM's participation in the AMA ban, however, the car was campaigned by Mitchell himself, with the ubiquitous Dick Thompson at the wheel. At its first outing at Marlboro, Maryland, in April 1959, Thompson managed fourth in spite of a temperamental braking system.

Thompson and the Sting Ray continued their romance throughout the 1959 and 1960 seasons, consistently finishing in the top ten, often dueling for first. And all this was accomplished by Mitchell's own small racing team, with the implicit but silent blessing of GM management.

Despite the AMA ban, production Corvettes were also being raced, even if it was without Chevrolet's direct involvement. In 1960, for instance, American enthusiast Briggs Cunningham took a three-car team to Le Mans. Only one of the cars finished, with drivers John Fitch and New York car dealer Bob Grossman taking a credible eighth overall in their Corvette.

In America, the privateers were doing well too, thanks to the 1962 introduction of a larger, 327 ci V-8. With 360 hp in fuel-injected form and 340 hp with carburetors, Corvettes dominated SCCA A-Production and B-Production racing, with drivers such as Jim Jeffords, Dick Thompson, Don Yenko, Bob Johnson, Bob Bondurant, Dave MacDonald, Dick Guldstrand and Paul Reinhart confronting the challenges put forth by Jaguar, Mercedes and Ferrari. It was a great year for racing Corvettes, with Dick Thompson winning

a national championship in A-Production, Don Yenko in B-Production, and a host of other drivers capturing regional championships.

Good as it was, Chevrolet hoped it would get even better. Little did anyone know at the time, but the body of Bill Mitchell's Sting Ray racer was actually the predecessor of the all-new 1963 production Corvette Sting Ray. With a new look and a new chassis, the Sting Ray dramatically opened a new era in Corvette history. As if its design was not sufficiently exciting—especially with the new fastback body style—its engine and chassis delivered on the performance promised by its proportions.

The Sting Ray was the first Corvette with independent rear suspension, replacing the leaf springs and live axle used previously. Many options were new for the year, including power windows and power steering, but tucked at the bottom of the option list was something quite special: option Z06. At first glance, the Z06 package looked like nothing more than a bunch of heavy-duty parts, a reworded equivalent of the RPO 684 competition option first offered in 1957. Closer inspection revealed that it was enough to turn the average Corvette into an all-out racer. For a total of $1,818.14, those in the know could obtain a Sting Ray coupe with the top fuel-injected 360 hp 327 ci V-8; power-assisted, ventilated, heavy-duty brakes with sintered metallic linings; heavy-duty front stabilizer bar, heavy-duty shock absorbers and springs; a Positraction rear axle; and a 36½ gallon fiberglass fuel tank. Knock-off wheels were also part of the option, but porosity problems delayed introduction until the 1964 model year. Chevrolet wasn't fooling anybody, of course. These Sting Rays were destined to be raced.

---

**Arkus-Duntov had worked to make the Corvette competitive on the racetrack, and he was not about to let Shelby put one over on his real McCoy.**

---

According to Corvette archaeologist Noland Adams, the first crop of Z06 equipped Corvettes were sold only to drivers with proven racing records. Their first competition appearance took place at Riverside, California, for the fifth annual *Los Angeles Times* Grand Prix for Sports Cars on the weekend of October 12, 1962. One of the richest sports car races in the world, the *Times* Grand Prix attracted the finest drivers and cars along with record crowds. The Three Hour Invitational Race in which the Corvettes were set to run was scheduled for Saturday prior to the Grand Prix on Sunday. Four Z06s were present, so new that their break-in mileage was the distance between St. Louis and Los Angeles. They were assigned to well-known West Coast drivers Dave MacDonald, Bob Bondurant, Doug Hooper and Jerry Grant. Considering the combination of power and talent brought together in the Z06, there was much pride in the Corvette camp.

No one, however, counted on Carroll Shelby. His new Cobra would change the face of big-bore production racing forever.

## Cobra challenger

When the first two Cobra prototypes were completed at Dean Moon's shop in Santa Fe Springs, California, it was decided to enter one of them in the *Times* Invitational race. Bill Krause, a recognized West Coast Modified driver, was selected to pilot the car. At first he appeared to be engaging in a lopsided battle: four powerful Corvettes against the lone, unproven Cobra prototype. It was not long before David showed up Goliath.

---

**When Arkus-Duntov first saw the Cobra leaving his Corvette in its wake, he remarked, "The handwriting is on the wall." Fortunately, he had already deciphered it.**

---

After a fierce early lap battle with MacDonald's Corvette, Krause and the Cobra ran away from the Corvettes. Well on his way to an easy win, Krause was sidelined when his left rear wheel hub broke. Doug Hooper, driving speed-part manufacturer Mickey Thompson's Z06 Corvette, won the race in the only one of the four Z06s to finish. "I don't think it's ever been done before, a new production car winning the first time out," said the jubilant Thompson. But his enthusiasm was premature.

Shortly thereafter, at Riverside once again, the Cobras firmly demonstrated their superiority. Dave MacDonald and Ken Miles trounced the Corvettes so securely that Miles even pitted unnecessarily, waited for the Corvettes to pass, and then set about catching up, until the lead Corvette was relegated to third place.

What went wrong with the Corvettes? One problem, as usual, was braking, as the Z06's sintered linings were useless until warmed up. "The first time I drove the car," recalled Doug Hooper for *Automobile Quarterly*, "we found out how terrible the brakes were. When I hit the brakes, I almost went over the guard rail. The car would pull violently either to the right or the left and never do the same thing twice."

The other problem was weight, pure and simple. The typical Z06 Sting Ray weighed some 3,100 pounds, while the bantamweight Cobra tipped the scales at just 2,000 pounds. And in spite of the Corvette's more sophisticated suspension and higher horsepower, the Cobra's weight still gave it a distinct advantage. "The Cobra's lightness," concluded *Road & Track* in a June 1963 comparison of the two cars, "allows it to accelerate and corner faster, and stop quicker (primarily due to the advantage provided by its disc brakes), and on a straightaway of a likely length, the Cobra will be a good 10-mph faster."

It has been said that when Zora Arkus-Duntov first saw the Cobra prototype leaving his Corvette in its wake, he remarked, "The handwriting is on the wall."

Fortunately, he had already deciphered it.

While Chevrolet was busy building and testing the new Corvette Sting Ray in mid-1962, another interesting project was taking place in a small shop in Santa Fe Springs, California, above. This was Carroll Shelby's first Cobra, and he decided to introduce the car in the Three Hour Invitational enduro prior to the *Los Angeles Times* Grand Prix on October 14, 1962. Ironically, this was also to be the racing debut of the 1963 Corvette Sting Ray.

**Riverside, October 1962**
After a Le Mans start on the back straight, the race became a wheel-to-wheel duel, left, between Dave MacDonald in the Don Steves' Corvette Z06 (00) and Bill Krause in the Shelby Cobra. Gradually Krause pulled out to a half-lap lead, before both he and MacDonald retired with broken left rear wheels. The handwriting was on the wall; big-bore production racing had changed forever in the course of one afternoon.

The win was taken by Doug Hopper in Mickey Thompson's Z06 (119), left. As the jubilant Thompson crew celebrated, Zora Arkus-Duntov realized that "something must be done quickly." Thus the plan to build a lightweight Corvette was given the green light by Chevrolet General Manager Bunkie Knudsen.

The forerunner of the Grand Sport was the Corvette Super Sport of 1956, shown here at left in a rare contemporary photo, unfortunately out of focus. The story of the SS read much like that of the Grand Sport— and could have served as an omen. Zora Arkus-Duntov embarked on experimental project XP–64 in an attempt to win racing laurels for his baby. Chevrolet's acceptance of the 1957 AMA ban on racing derailed the SS; the same ban was the thorn in the side of the Grand Sport almost seven years later. *Automobile Quarterly*

Bill Mitchell's 1960 Sting Ray racer, below, was the missing link between the Corvette SS and the Grand Sport. Based on the extra Super Sport "mule" chassis, it wore futuristic body work that foreshadowed the 1963 production Corvette. And like the Grand Sport, the Sting Ray's engine breathed through four exotic Italian Weber carburetors. The XP–87, as it was called in factory parlance, won the SCCA C-Modified championship in 1960, the most prestigious laurels won by any factory Corvette special. *Automobile Quarterly*

**Riverside, October 1962**
During an early practice session for the race, Bill Krause, in the new Cobra, is discussing the handling characteristics of the car with Carroll Shelby, above. The XP on the side of the Cobra stood for Experimental Production; it was the designation for a special production class of cars that had not reached the minimum number of units to be classified as production cars under SCCA rules.

# Chapter 2

# Birth of the Grand Sport

At just about the moment the Cobras promised to run off and hide from the Corvettes at Riverside, Chevrolet was putting the finishing touches on the volley it would launch at its crosstown rival.

In early 1962, Zora Arkus-Duntov and an elite group of Chevrolet engineers were given the green light by Chevrolet boss Bunkie Knudsen to begin work on a lightweight Sting Ray. The timing was ideal for such a car; the Federation Internationale de l'Automobile (FIA)—the international organization that controlled road racing—had begun to put a heavy emphasis on its production-based Grand Touring classification. The shift, according to *Car and Driver's* Stephen Wilder, came because the FIA "was less interested in generating the wild-eyed excitement of the sports-racing game . . . than in keeping road-racing alive in an environment that remembers all too clearly the Le Mans disaster of 1955." With the spotlight now on production sports cars, it meant that the FIA's Championship of Manufacturers would go to the Cobra, making it the first American car to capture this honor. And no one at Chevrolet—least of all Knudsen—wanted that to happen.

## Birth of the Lightweight

First, Knudsen had to have a car that could compete. It had become apparent long before the Sting Ray's racing debut at Riverside that its foremost problem was weight. Arkus-Duntov's goal was to build a Corvette that could take on the Cobra pound for pound; that meant getting the weight of the car down to 2,000 pounds—or about 1,100 pounds less than the production Sting Ray. It would not be easy.

At the time, Chevrolet—unlike Ford—was still paying lip service to the 1957 AMA ban on racing, so work on the new Corvette racer was carried out in utter secrecy within the Chevrolet Engineering Center. Although it became known officially as the Grand Sport—right down to the fabrication of a specific badge—most simply referred to it as the "Lightweight."

In order to get around the AMA agreement, wrote author Paul Van Valkenburgh in *Chevrolet=Racing . . . ?*, Chevrolet planned to build 125 cars for FIA homologation and then sell them to amateur drivers around the country. All those drivers needed, wrote Van Valkenburgh, "was the basic raw material, and Chevrolet would not have to get involved with factory support."

The basic raw material, as Zora Arkus-Duntov saw it, was a purpose-built racer that would weave a delicate line between the AMA dictate and the needs of the racing marketplace. It started with a new frame, the responsibility of which fell to Walter Zetye, who, along with Arkus-Duntov and Harold Krieger, had patented the 1963 production Corvette's rear suspension. With insufficient time to develop a space frame similar to that of the SS to fit under the Sting Ray's new body, Zetye's team—including future Cadillac Chief Engineer Bob Dorn—opted instead for a ladder-type chassis constructed with massive tubular members extending from front to rear. The tubes were made of seamless steel and not aluminum as some reports have suggested. These members were connected at the front and back with cross-members of approximately the same diameter, while another tube crossed the middle of the chassis, directly aft of the transmission. A fourth cross-member was installed just ahead of the rear kick-up and served as the anchor point for an integral roll cage.

With Daytona and Sebring coming up the following February and March respectively, the pressing schedule left no time for testing the new chassis. At the last minute, however, someone discovered that the first chassis had been built ¼ inch short, so it was decided to test its strength on a pneumatic stroking machine that simulated overall torsional and beaming loads as well as brake reaction forces. The results were encouraging, as the tubular frame proved to be slightly stronger than its production car counterpart—and this despite being some ninety-four pounds lighter. "I must say that we found very little wrong," said Zetye. "We went through a 100,000 cycle test and there were very few things that we had to fix."

Given that the Corvette had just received an all-new suspension layout, including an independent rear axle shared with no other GM product, the suspension geometry of the Lightweight approximated that of the production car. To minimize excess weight, however, production components were replaced with lighter, hand-built equivalents. For example, the production car's front upper and lower A-arms were stamped, while those on the Lightweight were fabricated from sheet steel. The slender knuckles that connected them were a work of art; made from a chrome-nickel-molybdenum alloy, they were, in the words of one engineer, "so hard that most of our tools couldn't machine them." To save additional weight, the trailing arms were drilled, which, together with an aluminum differential housing, shaved nearly 100 pounds from the rear axle. An aluminum steering box—containing faster, 14.0:1 gearing—helped cut eleven more pounds. More weight was saved with 15x6 inch Halibrand knock-off magnesium alloy wheels fitted with Firestone 6.50–15 Super Sports. Apparently Firestone was not foreseen as the unique tire supplier, as Goodyear also supplied a set of its 6.50–15 Stock Car Specials for evaluation.

The main chassis members ran directly under the Grand Sport's cockpit instead of alongside it, and thus the driving position had to be raised slightly in order for the body to maintain its relationship with the frame. This meant that the driver would sit slightly higher than in the production Corvette, but also that the body could easily be removed from the chassis. The body itself was also made lighter by using hand-laid pieces of woven fiberglass cloth. Further weight reduction was achieved by replacing the steel birdcage structure of the production car with one hand-fabricated from aluminum.

The appearance of the Grand Sport body generally duplicated that of the production coupe, although the rotating headlights of the production car were replaced with fixed versions under plexiglass covers. All windows except for the front windshield were made of plexiglass as well, and Design chief Bill Mitchell's prized split rear window divider was let go too—in the interest of weight savings as well as visibility.

Beneath the one-piece rear window lay a 36½ gallon fiberglass fuel tank, positioned slightly forward of the production car's because FIA regulations demanded a spare tire and a vestigial trunk. This meant that the fuel filler was relocated to the right-hand sail panel. Inside, the production car's twin-eyebrow dash was carried over, complete with an instrument panel that included a 200 mph speedometer. Custom racing seats were fabricated, along with rudimentary door panels and window lifts. As an example of the thoroughness of its diet, the Grand Sport's completed doors weighed just twenty-one pounds apiece. Although lacking any other interior trim, the cockpit was fully carpeted.

The weakness of the Corvette's drum brakes had been apparent since its earliest racing days. Even the sophisticated system developed for the SS couldn't cope with the Corvette's combination of high speed and heavy weight. This made the development of

The stock Corvette script and the special Grand Sport bar logo as mounted on the rear trunk lid of a Grand Sport coupe. The twist nut in the bottom right corner of the photo was to hold the trunk lid secure. *Maggie Logan*

four-wheel discs for the Grand Sport a top priority. Project Engineer Ashod Torosian, himself a veteran of the SS project, was given charge of finding the best binders available.

"At the time we started this project," said Torosian, "the only disc brakes Delco had were dreams—they existed only on paper. We looked at the Dunlop systems, and investigated the brakes on the D-Type Jaguar." To test their suitability to the Corvette, explained Torosian, "we built up a 1961 prototype with a Bendix-Dunlop system, but it didn't have the capacity we needed." That was hardly surprising, since the D-Type weighed about 1,000 pounds less than a production 1961 Corvette.

Torosian then turned to Girling, which supplied larger, three-piston calipers that delivered greater clamping force than the Dunlops. Solid rotors were used front and rear, measuring 11¼ inches in diameter and ¾ inch thick. In order to maintain maximum braking power, a vacuum booster was specified.

While his team was working on the chassis, Arkus-Duntov was selecting a suitable engine. He began with the basic small-block architecture, substituting an aluminum block for the cast-iron original. Its initial displacement was set at 402 ci, achieved with an utterly square bore and stroke of four inches. Testing revealed that the longest stroke possible was 3¾ inches, which brought the total displacement down to 377 ci. To make the most of that displacement, a special hemispherical cylinder head was developed, permitting larger intake and exhaust valves. In addition, the heads were reworked to provide two spark plugs for each cylinder. On the dyno, the dual-plug 377 ci engine produced 550 hp at 6400 rpm with maximum torque of 500 lb-ft at 5200 rpm. "These were numbers with which to conjure," wrote Karl Ludvigsen. "No GT or sports-racer had yet been built with more power than this."

Arkus-Duntov's plans called for the initial construction of six cars, the first of which would be used as a development mule while the others were being assembled. The mule, chassis number 001, was completed on November 14, 1962. According to a preliminary weight comparison compiled in mid-November of that year, the Grand Sport's curb weight—with aluminum heads and exhaust manifolds—came in at 2,283 pounds, nearly 800 pounds lighter than the 3,062 pound production car. A slightly later report contained two different Grand Sport weight breakdowns, one labeled "as built" and another "competitive." The weight for the former was listed as 2,230 pounds, while the latter was 75½ pounds lighter because of the all-aluminum engine.

## Trial run at Sebring

About a month after the completion of the 001 mule, Arkus-Duntov and the first Grand Sport traveled to Sebring to test the brakes as well as other components. Handling the driving duties was Corvette pilot Dick Thompson, who had previously helped Arkus-Duntov sort out the chassis for the 327 engined 1962 Corvette, and Masten Gregory, fresh from that year's Nassau Speed Week.

Also present at Sebring was Ashod Torosian, who was there to work out any braking problems. Torosian recalled that Gregory and the "green" Grand Sport were able to lap the 4.5 mile Sebring circuit

18

with astonishing speed: "Gregory did about six laps and came within seconds of the track record. The thing that shocked me was that none of those six laps was higher than 3:17. That guy was so smooth." With Gregory's times so close to the 1962 track record, victory at Sebring was within Chevrolet's grasp.

---

> "We knew then that if we put the correct engine in the [Lightweight] we could win the race. We were that confident. . ."
> *Project Engineer Ashod Torosian*

---

The engine used in the mule was a modified L84 fuel-injected 327 ci fitted with several lightweight components, including flywheel, clutch and air filter. Contemporary records suggest that the test engine and a spare were fitted with aluminum heads and cast-aluminum exhaust manifolds, although it is not known if they were actually used during the testing. In spite of the production-based powerplant, however, the Grand Sport's performance was right on target. "We knew then that if we put the correct engine in the car," Torosian continued, "we could win the race. We were that confident of what we saw with Masten."

Confidence in the brakes, however, was still lacking. At one point, said Torosian, when Gregory came in for an inspection, "the front rotors were glowing. We were running Halibrand wheels with skinny Firestone tires. I looked through the holes and saw something glowing at me. We simply didn't have enough rotor capacity to go from 110 mph down to 30."

Upon his return to Warren, Michigan, Torosian went back to work on the rotors and after consulting with an aerospace engineer, discovered that they had insufficient mass. As a result, they were widened to one inch, while Chevrolet-developed internal ventilation channels helped increase heat dissipation.

The Sebring brake test was completed just prior to the 1962 Christmas holiday, and its results gave Arkus-Duntov and his team a certain optimism about their potential at Daytona and Sebring—and perhaps even Le Mans. Beyond the six cars already planned, work would soon begin on the homologation run of 125 cars, twenty-five more than the FIA requirement just to show that Chevrolet was serious, unlike Ferrari which had failed to produce the required number of GTOs demanded by the FIA.

But there was more to it. Many were confident that the Lightweight would be for Chevrolet what the Cobra was for Ford: a sports racer that would stimulate demand for a slightly tamer—though no less tough—street version. After the first 125 cars were built, so the thinking went, an additional 1,000 street Grand Sports might follow. "We thought that it was going to be a 'go' program," recalled Torosian. At about that time, Chevrolet had just acquired a plant at Mound and 9 Mile roads in Warren to produce Corvette torque arms; the labor-intensive Grand Sport production line would be set up there.

Hardly had the New Year been rung in when the dreams of Christmas Eve were squelched by the realities of corporate life. News of the Sebring test—and likely its promising results—had reached the fourteenth floor and the desk of GM Chairman Frederic Donner. The word came back in no uncertain terms that no GM division would be permitted to stray from the AMA racing ban, period.

At the time, Torosian was preparing to leave for another Sebring test trip, his bags packed. On the afternoon of January 5, 1963, he got a telephone call from Arkus-Duntov with the bad news. "We were planning to go back to Sebring after New Year's," he remembered. "I had my money and my ticket all ready. Zora called at about 4:00 pm and told me that during the holiday, the program had been canceled."

Fortunately for the Grand Sport team, enough parts had been fabricated to build five complete cars; although many documents from the early stages of the Grand Sport project refer to six cars, later evidence indicates conclusively that only the five were ultimately assembled. At least three of the cars were completed by the start of the 1963 racing season. And even though Chevrolet was not going to "produce" any Grand Sports, that did not prevent them from loaning the existing cars to friendly outsiders—without any direct assistance, of course.

## The Grand Sport premiere

While GM was doing its best to dismantle the Grand Sport project, the Shelby Cobras promised to walk away with the 1963 season. At Riverside in February, Ken Miles was so far out in front of the overweight Z06s that he pitted for nothing more than a glass of water, exiting to pass all of the Corvettes and finish a close second to teammate MacDonald.

In the meantime, a completed Grand Sport, chassis number 003, was loaned to Dundee, Illinois, Chevrolet dealer Dick Doane; Grand Sport 004 was also lent to Gulf Oil Research executive Grady Davis. Davis' primary driver would be Dick Thompson, while Doane would drive his car himself.

Because the Grand Sports had never reached production status, they ran in the C-Modified class, racing against such full-scale racing machinery as Lance Reventlow's Scarab and Jim Hall's Chaparral—and they did so with normal, iron-block 360 hp fuel-injected 327 ci engines. According to Thompson, this was a calculated step by Arkus-Duntov, who didn't want judgment passed on the cars, as they had had so little development. "They would give us nothing but production engines," Thompson said. "Zora didn't want [the aluminum-block 377 ci engine] run, because it wasn't ready."

Davis' car 004 was the first to see action, starting at the SCCA season opener at Marlboro on April 7, 1963. The understated white car was the star of the paddock, but Thompson was held back when a faulty fuel injector left him standing on the starting grid. At Danville, Virginia, on April 28, Ed Lowther stood in for Thompson and finished fourth overall, third in class. In May at Cumberland, Maryland, Thompson returned to the wheel and finished fifth overall, third in class. And at the June Sprints, at Road America,

Elkhart Lake, Wisconsin, Thompson diced it out with Andy Devine's Scarab to finish third in class once again.

The situation deteriorated during the summer months, as the car failed to finish at Lake Garnett, Kansas, and Meadowdale, Illinois. For Thompson, the latter event was particularly memorable: "The car didn't handle properly because of its aerodynamics," he recalled. "At Meadowdale, I experienced a car that actually flew. As I crested a hill, the next thing I knew I was looking up in the air! It came down with a big bang and broke both shock mounts."

---

*"I experienced a car that actually flew. As I crested a hill, the next thing I knew I was looking up in the air!"*
*Driver Dick Thompson*

---

Following the Meadowdale debacle, the Davis car was given a new twin-inlet Rochester fuel-injection system; its presence was manifested by an oversized mailbox-like air scoop on the hood that supplemented a smaller scoop added after Road America.

The revamped Davis car 004 appeared at the SCCA Nationals at Watkins Glen, New York, in late August. The revisions it received paid off handsomely, as Thompson took an overall victory and turned in the highest average speed of the day, 90.8 mph. But that would be the end of the spoils for the 1963 season: at Bridgehampton the following month, Thompson was sidelined with brake problems. Nonetheless, he managed to finish the season fourth in C-Modified, not bad at all for an unproven car lacking any form of factory support.

While the Davis/Thompson car competed several times during the 1963 season, the Doane Grand Sport 003 showed up in only two events. At Meadowdale, where Thompson did not finish, Dick Doane co-drove his car to a sixth-place finish. At the Road America 500 in September, Doane, alone this time, did his best to keep ahead of a competitive field of Cobras, Elva-Porsches and Lotuses. He prevailed for ninety-three laps, ultimately succumbing to a blown engine.

Interestingly, there was scant contemporary press coverage of the cars in 1963, but then no one at Chevrolet would probably reveal much about them. *Car Life,* in its August 1963 issue, referred to it as the "Never-never Corvette," and alluded to the fact that Arkus-Duntov had done his best during the Sebring brake test to keep the lid on everything. "There was an incredible amount of information disseminated about these tests," said *Car Life's* Bob Harrison. "Most of it was due to wishful thinking, probably, but Duntov's refusal to release accurate information also greatly aggravated the error."

Although the wins in 1963 were few, much had been learned, and while the two early cars were on the track, Arkus-Duntov was constantly monitoring them and modifying the cars that had been held back at Warren. In October 1963, he recalled his two scouts, aware that the firepower they needed was lacking. He knew what was required, and by the time the Nassau Speed Week came around in December, so too would the Cobra team.

Zora Arkus-Duntov, far left, discusses the new Corvette Sting Ray. As the new production Corvette was being introduced, plans had already been laid for a lightweight, Grand Touring version. Arkus-Duntov was adamant that Chevrolet needed to do something to confront Shelby's Cobra; the Lightweight would do just that. As with his counterparts at Jaguar and Porsche, Arkus-Duntov believed that endurance racing was the ultimate test of an automobile and he yearned to compete. *Road & Track photo.* As the head of Chevrolet Motor Division, S. E. "Bunkie" Knudsen, left, felt sufficiently independent of the AMA ban to give Arkus-Duntov the green light to begin work on the Grand Sport project. But when GM Chairman Frederic Donner decided to clamp down on racing, it was Knudsen who took the heat for Chevrolet's "high performance experiments," and was ultimately responsible for disbanding the Grand Sport program.

The first Grand Sport chassis begins to take shape in a windowless back room at Chevrolet Engineering, left. The frame was built of seamless steel tubes instead of the production 1963 Sting Ray's square-section beams. The longitudinal frame rails were 4.25 in. in diameter while the front cross-member was five inches to take the weight of the front suspension load. The outriggers at the front of the chassis, as seen in the lower right, were for the radiator. Moving back, the number two cross-member supporting the transmission was four inches in diameter; number three was 4.25 in.; and number four was four inches. The layout of the Grand Sport framework followed a similar, albeit abbreviated design to that of the production model, although the Lightweight's frame was exactly that—lightweight.

A close-up view, above left, of the Grand Sport's right rear body mount and rear cross-members. The strength of the seamless-steel-tube frame is obvious here. The framework has been painted gloss black. The front suspension, steering links and Girling disc brake are seen above right. The brake caliper is aluminum and the disc is 11¼ inches in diameter. The large diameter coil springs and Delco high-performance shocks are also visible here, as is the steering box, top right. The battery box is at far left. A Grand Sport chassis undergoes a stress test on one of the Chevrolet stroking machines, right. Pneumatic cylinders pound the suspension up and down, while an air motor torques the driveline. Results were good. The engineers' target was to have the frame strong enough to handle 2,500 lb-ft of torque per degree of twist. Note that this chassis is unpainted, showing off the weld seams in the tubing.

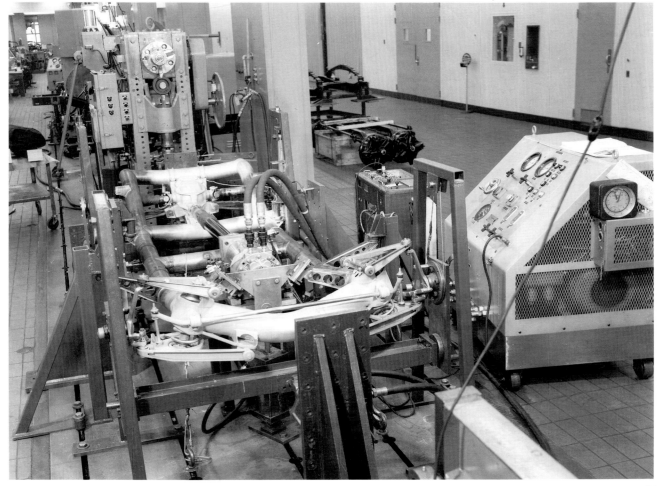

An overhead view of the right front suspension and brake, above left. These solid discs were soon replaced with vented discs for better cooling. A good view of the frame, left, looking directly toward the rear from front dead center; note white line on the front cross-member indicating dead center. Steering arms and lightweight steel suspension components are plainly visible here. Stands holding the frame off the ground had to be carefully placed to avoid damaging these special parts. Engineers are at work on an engine in the back of the shop. Looking forward from the rear centerline shows the special aluminum differential housing, above. Stronger halfshafts than the production car's units were used, mounted through special lightweight radius arms. Note that the rear transverse spring design was similar to that of the production Corvette and the Cobra; it is attached to the rear end by four bolts and to the radius arms using large rubber grommets. The body mounts and large diameter frame tubes are also visible here.

The 36½ gallon fiberglass gas tank has been installed here, along with the driveshaft, above. The gas tank was mounted considerably forward of that of the production car for improved weight distribution. Note that many of the frame components have been drilled to reduce unnecessary weight. The hand brake is visible as well as the shift lever. The first Grand Sport nears the point at which the body will be attached, right. The number 1 is written on the rear left mainframe member. The Rochester fuel-injected, 327 ci, 360 hp engine has been installed, complete with aluminum bellhousing and transmission case. The magnesium alloy knock-off wheels are by Halibrand. The Grand Sport was one of the last racing cars to be designed and built around "skinny" tires. The spare tire was not to be used and was on the car merely to meet race rules. The spare here is a Goodyear; the other tires are Firestone Super Sports 6.50/6.70–15. The Grand Sports' aluminum birdcage was handmade and formed the cage around the doors and windows, above right. Note the weight, 23 lbs, inscribed on the cross-member.

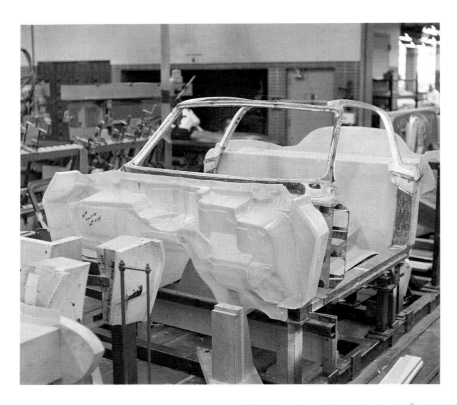

The aluminum framework has been set in place and the fiberglass central armature is beginning to take shape, above. The fiberglass armature is much abbreviated from the production cars'. At one time word swept through the racing world that Chevrolet was building an "aluminum-bodied Corvette." A false rumor. The fiberglass body has been installed on the first Grand Sport, right. The body was made in one piece—not including doors, trunk lid and hood—and could be lifted on and off of the chassis as a single unit. The right-side gas filler cap is visible just behind the passenger door. Left three-quarter rear view of the first Grand Sport, above right. The fiberglass body was specially molded and laid up by hand. Although most of the body at least resembled stock body panels, the fiberglass was much thinner and lighter. The body was 0.06 in. thick using three layers of fiberglass cloth; the production car was 0.10 in. thick, using five-layer fiberglass. All windows, except for the front windshield, were made of plexiglass. The reported weight of the car was thus as low as 2,000 pounds.

Front view of the first Grand Sport body, above right. Note the vents behind the front wheels as on production 1963 Sting Rays. The Grand Sport hood, however, was minus the twin louvers of the production model although the inset panels for the louvers were molded into the hood. The headlamps are fixed in position with a clear plexiglass shield covering them; production cars had rotating covers. One major difference, right, from the production model Corvette was the installation of the trunk as required by the FIA; production cars had no such trunk, and stored the spare wheel in a rack below the rear section of the car. FIA rules dictated that there had to be space for a spare wheel *and* a suitcase. The spare here now wears a Firestone tire. The one-piece rear plexiglass window is visible here as compared with the famous split rear window of the 1963 Sting Ray. Also note the bolts on the underside of the trunk lid that hold in place the Corvette script and Grand Sport logo.

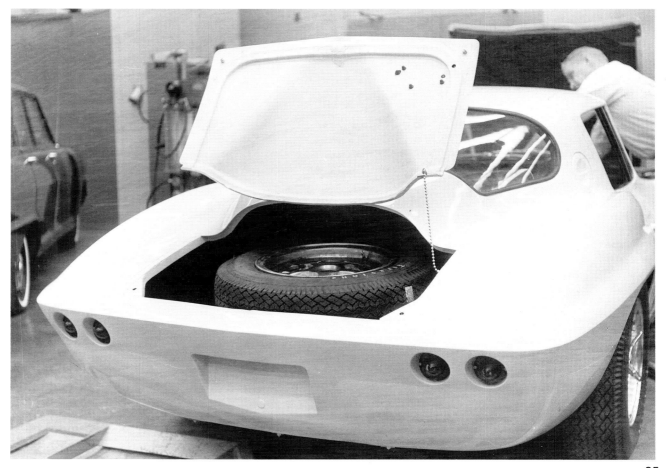

The interior of the Grand Sport looked like a production model with subtle changes, above. The absence of hardware on the door is obvious; the strap is for raising and lowering the side window, and the knob is for opening the door. The dashboard was unupholstered with only a small metal plaque at the center console's base indicating shift pattern. The driver's seat was adjustable but the passenger seat was fixed in place. The Grand Sport received the standard steering wheel and dash, right. The only changes to the instrumentation were the substitution of an oil temperature gauge for the gasoline gauge and the addition of a 200 mph speedometer. The turn signal indicator holes are vacant.

Chevrolet mechanic Ernie Loomis works on the 001 Grand Sport's engine in front of one of Sebring's famous hangars, above. Note the standard Sting Ray in the background: one of the early 1963 cars.

The first serious test of the Grand Sport took place at Sebring in mid-December 1962, left. The drivers were Dick Thompson and Masten Gregory, and the goal was to test brakes and tires, and to send the car through a thorough shakedown. This test was shielded from GM executives, as the Grand Sport was accompanied to Sebring by several production and experimental Sting Rays. The famous Grand Sport front-end lift is obvious already as the right front wheel is about to come off the ground. This lifting problem was really never cured and became a signature of the Grand Sport when it was under heavy acceleration. Another problem was the overheating of the brakes. This was corrected by installation of vented discs and wider rotors.

Zora Arkus-Duntov, far left in photo at right, in conversation with Dick Thompson (dark clothes with helmet) and others. The Sebring tests were successful, and plans were made to enter the actual race in March 1963. But too much information leaked out, and GM management announced in January that the Grand Sport program was to be terminated at once.

**Riverside, February 1963**
As GM was cracking down on high-performance violations, the Shelby Cobra enjoyed its first runaway victory at an SCCA race at Riverside Raceway in February 1963. Ken Miles (98), shown leading Paul Reinhart's Corvette (6) and Dave MacDonald's Cobra (198), rubbed it in by making a pit stop for a glass of water. Exiting the pits in last place, he caught and passed all of the Corvettes and finished a close second to teammate MacDonald.

As executive vice president of Gulf Oil, Grady Davis was a devoted Corvette supporter, sponsor and—on occasion—a driver, too. Davis bought Grand Sport 004 from Chevrolet and campaigned it in 1963.

**Marlboro, Maryland, April 1963**
The Corvette Grand Sport finally made its racing debut at the first SCCA Championship Race, at Marlboro, Maryland, on April 7, 1963. The car here is chassis number 004, and was driven by Dick Thompson and "owned" by Gulf Oil's Grady Davis. Davis is at left in straw hat, white pants and white jacket. At Marlboro the car drew a lot of attention, but stalled on the starting grid due to a faulty fuel injector. The car was painted white with a broad blue stripe.

A Washington, D.C., dentist by trade, Dick Thompson remains racing's most respected Corvette driver based on a winning career that began in 1956. Through his relationship with Grady Davis, he became involved with Grand Sports as early as the 1962 Sebring brake test. He later drove Grand Sports for Davis in the 1963 season, and for Roger Penske at Sebring in 1966.

**Marlboro, Maryland, April 1963**
One of the changes made to the 004 Grand Sport after the Sebring test was the addition of a small spoiler running across the front of the hood to help keep the front end down. Additional downforce would be needed as development proceeded. Note here the blank trays on the hood where the false louvers were glued onto production cars.

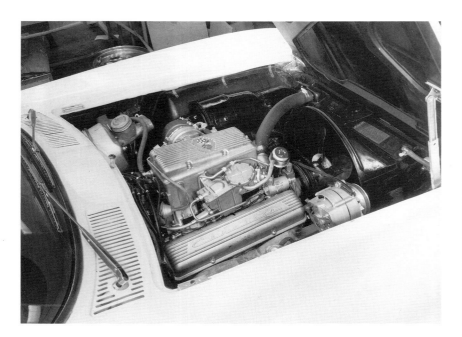

**Marlboro, Maryland, April 1963**
The engine, above left, as raced in Grand Sport 004 during the early 1963 season, was a stock L84 327 ci, 360 hp fuel-injected Corvette V–8. More post-Sebring modifications can be seen here on 004, above. The scoops on the top of the rear fenders were added to cool the rear brakes and the slots on the bottom of the rear fenders were added to help cool the differential. Once the fuel-injector problem was fixed, Thompson re-entered the race, and found that he was three to four seconds slower than winner Roger Penske's Cooper-Monaco. The biggest problem faced by the Grand Sport was having to run in the competitive C-Modified against such outright sports racers as Lance Reventlow's Scarab and Jim Hall's front-engined Chaparral. The Grand Sport was designed to be a production racer but was never homologated.

**Del Mar, California, April 1963**
It was also in April of 1963 that Corvette fans got something to cheer about, left. At an SCCA race in Del Mar, California, smooth-driving Paul Reinhart beat the Shelby American Cobra factory entry of Dave MacDonald (98). This was to be the only Cobra team loss to a production Corvette in 1963.

## Road America, June 1963

By the time the Davis/Thompson Grand Sport 004 arrived at Road America for the June Sprints, left, it had run in two more races. Ed Lowther stood in for Thompson at Danville, Virginia, and finished fourth overall, third in class, despite having some valve problems that limited the power of the car. Thompson again took over at Cumberland, Maryland, in May and finished fifth overall, third in class. At Road America, which always drew large crowds, the car was again the center of attention. The hood had been modified once more to accommodate a small scoop on the right side to help cool the engine compartment, while the original lateral spoiler was cut in half. The Grady Davis crew changes the brake pucks under the watchful eye of the crowd, below left. Note that the plexiglass headlamp covers have been replaced by fiberglass covers; an electronic tachometer has been mounted on top of the dash. Had the stock cable-driven tach failed?

## Road America, June 1963

In the 100 mile main event at the Road America June Sprints, left, Thompson got off to a great start and led a number of top cars for the early part of the race. Thompson (11) is leading Don Devine's Scarab (24), Hap Sharp's Cooper Monaco (93), Gates' Apache Roadster (28), Augie Pabst's Lotus 19 (7), Hansen's Chaparral (81) and Helson's Lister (12). As the field begins to sort itself out, below, Thompson still leads the pack. The Grand Sport is running in fast company here, leading Devine in the Scarab, Penske's Zerex Special (6), and Sharp. Penske, however, is about to take the lead, which he held until retiring with an oil leak.

**Road America, June 1963**

Thompson comes in for a pit stop to take on fuel and oil, right. Pit stops were much more casual in 1963, as Thompson doesn't even exit the car during refueling. Grady Davis, in his famous straw hat, is rushing to fuel the car. Thompson has two fingers up asking if he's running in second place; he finished third. Note here that the front hood doesn't seem to fit well as it is raised crooked. Thompson slides through a corner, below, in an effort to stay ahead of Hap Sharp's Cooper Monaco. Sharp was a DNF.

**Road America, June 1963**
The battle for second place between Devine's Scarab and Thompson was a dandy. When Thompson made his pit stop for fuel and oil, Devine took over second place for good. Thompson finished third overall and Harry Heuer in his Chaparral was the overall winner.

**Road America, June 1963**
Thompson's Grand Sport brakes and takes the Mecom Lotus 19 of Augie Pabst on the inside. Thompson's performance at Road America was outstanding considering that Chevrolet gave the car little support and few spare parts.

As the 1963 season wore on, it became more apparent that the Cobras were going to sweep all that was before them, above. The talent was exceptional: Bob Bondurant (99), Dan Gurney (97) and Lew Spencer (98); Bob Holbert and Ken Miles were also on the roster. No one could stop them.

**Watkins Glen, August 1963**
Grady Davis, far left in photo above right, and his crew take time out for a few laughs during a break in the action. In the foreground (in white coveralls) is Davis' crew chief Don Yenko. Bill Hartley, the engine builder, is in the background. Dick Thompson watches as Grand Sport 004 is unloaded at the Watkins Glen SCCA National on August 24, 1963, right.

**Watkins Glen, August 1963**
Just prior to the Watkins Glen race, Grand Sport 004 underwent some changes—again. The car was given a complete overhaul, top left, a large hood scoop was added to feed air to a new downdraft induction system composed of two Rochester air metering venturis, and the inside of the front fenders was cut away to relieve heat buildup in the engine compartment. At the Watkins Glen National, Grand Sport 004 was competitive, top right, with Thompson leading from the start of the 30 lap main event. Halfway through the race, above, Thompson was passed by Harry Heuer's Chaparral (21), but on lap 27 the Chaparral lost its rear end and Thompson went on to chalk up the first victory for the Corvette Grand Sport.

**Watkins Glen, August 1963**
Thompson receives congratulations from the Grady Davis crew. Note the pit board: Beer Time. The new hood scoop is quite visible here. It appears that as the hood scoops got bigger, the hood spoiler got smaller.

**Watkins Glen, August 1963**
As the season progressed and changes were made, it is interesting to note that the driver's cockpit remained the same, above. Note that the driver's seat is well padded, while the passenger's seat is rather sparse. A fire extinguisher is mounted in the passenger leg bay. Dick Thompson talking to Grady Davis, who looks like the Grim Reaper in his overcoat, right. These two had one of the most successful partnerships in SCCA racing.

**Road America, September 1963**
Dick Doane made one of his rare appearances in "his" Corvette Grand Sport, chassis number 003, at the Road America 500 in September 1963, above. The car (29), fitted with a long-stroke engine and painted a light metallic blue, was never really in the hunt. Doane is shown here with the Wester/Erickson Elva-Porsche (27), Skip Hudson's Maserati Tipo 151 (93) and the Lotus 23 of Markley/Rader (43). Dick Doane chases an Elva and the Cobra of Johnson/Spencer, left. The Grand Sport ran for 93 laps before being sidelined with a blown engine. From this back view, the additional venting that Doane added to the back of the car to cool the rear end is visible. This modification was later made to all of the Grand Sports by Chevrolet.

**Road America, September 1963**
The Doane/Sayler Grand Sport is pushed away after blowing its engine on the ninety-third lap, right. This was the last appearance for Doane's 003 car prior to being returned to Chevrolet for its Nassau modifications.

During the 1963 season, former Corvette driver Bob Johnson became the absolute dominating force of SCCA big-bore production racing, below. No one could come close to his well-prepared Cobra. The Cobras became omnipotent, and it was not until 1969 that a Corvette would again win the SCCA A-Production National Championship.

**Bridgehampton, September 1963**
The 004 Grand Sport of Grady Davis made its final appearance under his racing banner at the Bridgehampton 500 on September 15, 1963, left. The car was a strong runner until it encountered terminal brake problems. Thompson leads Holbert's Cobra (99), Hudson's Ferrari 330LM Berlinetta (47) and Sesslar's Porsche (72). Note that the Corvette has lost its grille, presumably in the name of extra engine cooling. Later in the race, above, Thompson leads the Alfa Giulia Berlina of Theodoracopulos and the eventual winner, Walt Hansgen in the Cunningham Cooper-Buick.

**Bridgehampton, September 1963**
Thompson and Skip Hudson race through the sand dunes of Bridgehampton Raceway on Long Island, New York, above. Without the grille on the Grand Sport, the two airhorns are visible at left. The NART 330LM Berlinetta was one of only four produced; it has obviously had a shunt here. Dick Thompson swings through a controlled power slide, left, to stay ahead of the Cobra of Ken Miles. Miles went on to finish second in the GT category while Thompson was a DNF due to brake failure.

**Bridgehampton, September 1963**
A good look at the Grand Sport 004 in its final race on "skinny" tires. Note that the fake side vents behind the front wheel has been cut out and covered with mesh. After the Bridgehampton race this car was recalled to Chevrolet for extensive modification prior to the 1963 Nassau Speed Week. Dick Thompson finished fourth overall in the SCCA C-Modified class for the 1963 season.

Prior to the Davis/Thompson 004 Grand Sport's return to Chevrolet in the fall of 1963, its engine and unique Rochester fuel-injection system were removed by Gulf Oil and later sold. *Ed Lowther*

Close-up of the special dual-inlet Rochester fuel-injection mechanics and manifold. *Ed Lowther*

# Chapter 3

# Nassau invasion, 1963

In 1954, a flamboyant Pennsylvania promoter named Sherman "Red" Crise convinced the Bahamas Ministry of Tourism to host a series of races on the island of Nassau. Granted FIA status via the Royal Automobile Club, the Nassau Speed Week became a popular event among prominent team owners and drivers. Although its airfield-based course was far from state of the art, the balmy locale—along with Crise's free-spirited attitude—made it the ideal spot for motor racing between the seasons.

In preparation for each year's Speed Week, Crise would send out colorful updates on the upcoming races, replete with predictions, proclamations and just plain gossip. Prior to the 1963 event, his flimsies focused on the promise of the Cobra entries and alluded to GM's reluctance to do anything about them. In November, however, an official press release from the Bahamas News Bureau suggested that all was not what it appeared: "A report persists that General Motors, which does not enter international road races, will not be completely disinterested in this one . . . Usually reliable sources say that three GM powered cars have been prepared especially for Speed Weeks."

In spite of GM's corporate ban on any official involvement with competition Corvettes—and its total cancellation of any plans for series production of the Grand Sports—there were still many within Chevrolet who felt that the Division should do something to derail the Cobra Express that had completely dominated the road-racing scene in 1963. With Chevrolet boss Knudsen's secret blessing, Arkus-Duntov set about giving Ford a dose of its own medicine at Nassau.

## The John Mecom Racing Team

Arkus-Duntov's ally in this somewhat treacherous endeavor was Texan John Mecom, the young and ambitious scion of a wealthy Houston family. Described by an acquaintance as "the nicest, most gentlemanly man you'd ever meet," Mecom's wealth precluded him from living a "normal" lifestyle. "His father wouldn't let him do anything," said the acquaintance. "He wouldn't let him play football. He'd let him own a polo pony, but he couldn't play polo."

One thing young Mecom *was* able to do was get involved with motor racing—as a team owner. In mid-1962, at age twenty-one, Mecom bought his first car and set about creating a top-notch team. To ensure success, he hired top drivers such as Roger Penske, Augie Pabst and A. J. Foyt. Thanks to his financial resources, he also had access to the best machinery—and mechanics to support it.

As a clean slate in the tangled world of corporate sponsorship, Chevrolet saw the Mecom Racing Team as the ideal third party to make an assault on the Cobras at Nassau without tipping its corporate hand. But first something would have to be done about the Grand Sports, only one of which—Grady Davis' 004—had managed a single victory during the 1963 season.

Following the Bridgehampton 500 in September, the Davis and Doane Grand Sports were recalled to Chevrolet, where they, along with a third car, chassis number 005, were treated to a complete makeover. Meanwhile, the 001 and 002 Grand Sports had remained with Chevrolet.

First, to take advantage of larger, low-profile Goodyear Stock Car Specials tires, the original 15x6 inch Halibrand wheels were replaced with beefier 9½-inch wide versions. This meant that the tires would now protrude outside the existing wheelhouses, so fender flares were added at the trailing edge of each wheelwell.

There were other body modifications as well, including a series of air vents across the rear filler panel to improve brake and differential cooling. Additional front brake and engine cooling was provided by opening up the normally decorative air scoops on the front fenders. And, as headlights would not be required in Nassau, they were masked with body-color covers.

Throughout the 1963 season, the Davis and Doane cars had raced with what was essentially a stock, iron-block 360 hp fuel-injected 327 ci engine. Even considering the Grand Sport's reduced weight, this engine was hardly on a scale with Arkus-Duntov's expectations.

For Nassau, he installed the full-race aluminum-block 377 ci engine that he had originally envisioned for the Grand Sports. Its fuel delivery system was changed to four Italian 58 mm DCOE Webers atop a cross-ram intake manifold in place of the Rochester fuel-injection system originally called for; single-plug aluminum heads were used in place of the dual-plug versions. According to writer Karl Ludvigsen, this engine was capable of 485 hp at 6000 rpm. To accommodate the taller induction system, special hoods were built with twin nostrils that further added to the menacing look of these second-generation Grand Sports.

The public's first glimpse of these cars came when the Mecom team—replete with the three Grand Sport Corvettes (003, 004, 005), a Lola-Chevy, a Cooper-Chevy, a rear-engined Scarab and the Zerex-Cooper Special—arrived in Nassau aboard the *Bahama Star* on November 30, 1963. When the three decidedly non-stock Sting Rays, each finished with Mecom's distinctive Cadillac Blue paint scheme, were unloaded from the hold, it didn't take long before everyone knew that something was up, especially Carroll Shelby and Ken Miles, who personally inspected the cars.

Denied any overt factory support, the Mecom team was, wrote Leo Levine in *Ford: The Dust and the Glory,* "accompanied by a group of Chevrolet engineers who coincidentally chose Nassau for a December vacation." The subterfuge didn't fool many. When rumors began circulating about the 377 ci engines, the Chevy officials insisted that they were in fact 327s.

To make the most of his mechanical equipe, Mecom had brought top-notch talent to drive the Grand Sports, including Jim Hall, Augie Pabst, Roger Penske and Dick Thompson. The Grand

The Mecom Racing Team shield. The logo carried a map of Texas with a red dot showing the Houston home base.

The map was flanked by a checkered flag on the left and the Texas state flag on the right, with Mecom Racing

Team written across the top. The colors were red, white, blue, silver and black.

Sport team was scheduled for three events, the ninety-nine-mile Tourist Trophy race on the first Sunday, followed by the 112 mile Governor's Cup on Friday and the 252 mile Nassau Trophy finale on the second Sunday.

According to tradition, the Tourist Trophy race was typically a Grand Touring event, which would normally have precluded the Grand Sport prototypes. But organizer Crise, in keeping with the spirit of the race, chose to bend the rules to allow the Chevy entries. "Like many another race organizer," reported Art Peck in *Road & Track*, "Red Crise doesn't care for the FIA thinking regarding GT emphasis and opened up the event to GT prototypes on a 'run for fun' basis."

The race itself was preceded by a five-lap qualifier, in which Mecom had entered two Grand Sports, car 005 driven by Thompson and car 003 by Hall. The pair qualified second and third respectively, earning the Corvettes front-row grid positions. They failed to make it through the main event, however, as both cars succumbed to unexpected rear-end difficulties due to insufficient differential cooling. The problem, it appeared, resulted from the fact that the ring and pinion gears were not sufficiently broken in, causing them to overheat and bind. During the following week, Mecom's team—with some help from a Chevrolet engineer who just happened to be going down to Nassau on short notice with an extra-heavy suitcase—worked to fix the rear axle problem. External differential oil coolers, adapted from passenger-car automatic transmission coolers, were installed on the rear deck just below the window.

---

"I was breathless with the stupendous acceleration of the car. If you really want to show off, you can leave rubber marks for a quarter mile. . ."
*Journalist Bernard Cahier*

---

All three cars were entered in the Governor's Cup on Friday. Penske was behind the wheel of 004, Thompson driving 005 and Augie Pabst—in his only Grand Sport ride—handling car 003. Penske took a respectable third, on the same lap as race winner A. J. Foyt in the Mecom Team Scarab. Pabst finished fourth and Dick Thompson, although not running at the finish, was scored sixth. That was a lot better than the Cobras, for the three Grand Sports had finished in the top ten while their Shelby adversaries were well back in the standings.

## Grand Sport versus Ferrari

The final event of the week was Sunday's Nassau Trophy race, and two Grand Sports were entered: car 005 driven by Dick Thompson and car 003 by Mecom newcomer John Cannon. Following the Le Mans-style dashing start, Penske ran off in the Mecom Cooper-Chevy, followed by Pedro Rodriguez in a works three-liter Ferrari 250P. Cannon and Thompson stayed within the top five, but soon found that air pressure building up in their engine compartments was threatening to pull the hoods free of their retainers. Pitting to tape them up cost them their lead, as Thompson finished fourth and Cannon eighth.

Throughout all three events, the Chevrolet-powered cars simply ran off from their Shelby rivals, a fact not lost on either camp. "The Chevrolet equipment won so easily," wrote Leo Levine, "there was even some embarrassment on the part of their factory personnel, who had hoped the journey south would escape unnoticed. But at the same time they were smirking. One of the engineers, when approached by a reporter with a technical question, laughed and said, 'You realize, of course, you're talking to a man who isn't here.'"

On the Monday after the race, John Mecom turned one of the cars over to journalist Bernard Cahier—one of the few times the Grand Sports turned up in the motoring press. Two of Cahier's major observations would be shared by virtually everyone who drove the cars. The upside was the tremendous acceleration: "I was breathless with the stupendous acceleration of the car . . . If you really want to show off, you can leave rubber marks for a quarter of a mile, as you still get wheel spin when putting it in third gear." But poor aerodynamics were the downside: "I noticed that at high speeds on the straight the combination of power, acceleration and the not-too-good aerodynamics of the car (it has an enormous frontal area) make the front of the car lift and the steering becomes light indeed."

Nonetheless, the Grand Sports had done what Knudsen and Arkus-Duntov desired—put the Cobra in its place. "The mission had been accomplished," said Levine. "Ford was shown it had a way to go."

Shelby was more sanguine. After the opening race on Monday, he flew off to London to get married, returning with his bride, Sue, on Wednesday. "Ah met her in New Zealand five years ago," he told *Road & Track*, "and told her to grow up and get the braces off her teeth and Ah'd marry her."

Buoyed by the Nassau results, the Grand Sports and their keepers returned to Warren, looking forward hopefully to the 1964 season, with Daytona, Sebring and perhaps Le Mans in sight.

**Nassau, 1963**

The first of the John Mecom Racing Team Grand Sports is lowered by boom from the hold of the *Bahama Star* at the quay in Nassau, above. Above right, a grinning John Mecom, left, and a youthful Roger Penske enjoy the moment as the Grand Sports are being unloaded from the *Bahama Star*. Some of the modifications to the "Sting Ray with hormones" are obvious here: a new hood design, wider front and rear fenders, wider Goodyear tires with deep-dish Halibrand wheels and the contoured headlight covers. At right, curious children gather around one of the Grand Sports at quayside; the boy on the left is offering some tuning help. Here is the reason for that new hood: the four massive Italian 58 mm Weber DCOE carburetors mounted on a special cross-ram manifold.

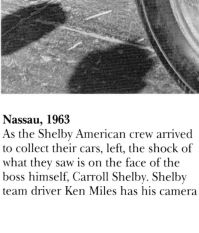

**Nassau, 1963**

As the Shelby American crew arrived to collect their cars, left, the shock of what they saw is on the face of the boss himself, Carroll Shelby. Shelby team driver Ken Miles has his camera ready. A concerned Shelby inspects the Grand Sport under the watchful eye of Miles and Corvette driver Roger Penske, above. As Shelby looks through the hood louvers, above right, an inquisitive Miles tries to question an evasive Roger Penske. Shelby's now on his hands and knees, right, inspecting the Grand Sport's suspension. The rest of the Cobra crew also satisfies its curiosity. Miles (still with his camera), is behind Shelby; Cecil Bowman (head above right fender) is next to Craig Lang, while Wally Peat is by the right rear fender looking through the window at the interior.

**Nassau, 1963**
John Mecom drives the first car from the pier, at left, followed by Roger Penske (12) in his car; Pabst drove the third car. The cars had to be driven through town on their way to the hangar that would serve as a giant communal garage. John Mecom, looking like the pied piper, leads his entourage through the center of town during business hours, above. Note that, while the tourists don't seem to care about the cars and the noise, the natives seem to relish all of the excitement.

Roger Penske, left, achieved instant international fame and success driving his controversial Zerex Special in major professional road races during the fall of 1962. He first drove the Grand Sport at Nassau in 1963 and continued driving it in 1964 with great success. Penske's keen business sense resulted in his retirement from driving at the end of the 1964 racing season, but he would return in 1966 as a team owner, buying the Grand Sport roadsters and racing 001 at Sebring.

At the tender age of 23, John Mecom, Jr., decided to go racing the right way, above. In late 1962, this young Houston oil scion put together a racing team to be reckoned with. He hired the best people, bought the best cars, and brought professionalism, class and style to American road racing. His wife, Catsy, left, did all of the team's scoring and timing.

A son of the famous Milwaukee brewing family, Augie Pabst, above, achieved his racing fame behind the wheels of the Scarabs and driving for the Briggs Cunningham and Mecom teams. He would have only one ride in a Grand Sport, at the Governor's Cup race at Nassau in 1963. Pabst was one of the great pranksters on the racing circuit in the sixties and gained everlasting fame for driving a Ford Falcon into the swimming pool of the Mark Thomas Inn in Monterey, California, during the Pacific Grand Prix weekend in 1961.

Jim Hall, right, is probably one of the greatest combination driver-engineer talents ever to grace the American racing scene, based on the engineering feats that were incorporated into his highly successful Chaparrals. His first drive in a Grand Sport was at Nassau in 1963 and he would co-drive with Penske on several occasions in 1964.

A true American racing legend and a winner in every type of racing he ever attempted, A. J. Foyt, above, would drive Grand Sports for John Mecom at Nassau and at Sebring in 1964.

The Nassau 1963 377 ci aluminum engine, above right, with its twin banks of Weber DCOE 58 mm carburetors. The use of aluminum castings and bronze fittings resulted in a glorious engine. This is a later picture of the sole remaining Nassau engine, owned by Jamey Mazzotta of Redding, California. Right, a bank of two Weber DCOE 58 carburetors on the remaining Nassau engine. *Maggie Logan*

**Nassau, 1963**
The engine, above, that powered the Grand Sports at Nassau sported a 377 ci aluminum cylinder block with aluminum heads. A special lightweight cross-ram manifold was designed to handle the 58 mm DCOE Weber carburetors. The carbs were bolted to the manifold in such a way that the two carbs on the right fed the left cylinders and the two carbs on the left side fed the right cylinders, hence the cross-ram name. The engine was light, simple and easy to repair. It was said to produce 435 lb-ft of torque at 4000 rpm and 485 hp at 6000 rpm.

**Nassau, 1963**
Visible on the left side of the Nassau Grand Sports are the vents in the front quarter panel, which served to cool the engine compartment and the front brakes, above right. The front fender flares are to cover the 15 inch front wheels and tires in accordance with FIA regulations.

**Nassau, 1963**
A number of the latest modifications are seen in this photo of the rear section of the car, right. The rear window is the one-piece plexiglass unit. The scoops on the fender and the louvers on the right rear of the fender are for cooling the rear brakes and the differential. The two marks on the gas filler cap indicate the locked and unlocked position at a quick glance; the cap is shown in the locked position. The fender flares were added to accommodate the 11 inch wide Halibrand wheels and latest low-profile Goodyear Stock Car Special tires.

A straight-on photo of the remaining Nassau engine, at left, showing the intricate throttle linkage operating the eight chokes. *Maggie Logan*

**Nassau, 1963**

The left quarter panel again shows the famous Grand Sport fender flares, above. Also visible here are the louvers cut in the rear fenders to cool the rear brakes and the massive four-inch exhaust pipe. The photograph at right was taken early on in the first weekend of racing action at Nassau and shows the "stock" configuration of the three Grand Sports as they arrived from Chevrolet. As problems developed during racing, oil coolers would be installed on the rear deck of each car to cool the differential.

**Nassau, 1963**
The three Grand Sport coupes parked in the huge hangar that served as a garage during Speed Week. The picture at left was taken early on since the race numbers have yet to be applied. Here, engine preparation is underway and fuel lines have yet to be hooked up to the carbs. Famed engine builder James Travers of Traco Engineering smokes a cigarette and tunes one of the 377 ci aluminum Grand Sport engines, below. Note that the one-piece fiberglass body has been lifted clear of the chassis for accessibility.

### Nassau, 1963
On December 1, 1963, the cars took to the potholed 4.5 mile track for the first practice laps, above. Lined up on the grid are the three Mecom Racing Team Grand Sports: Roger Penske in car 004 (50), Dick Thompson in car 005 (80) and Jim Hall in car 003 (65). Mecom was also running the Chevy-Lola (00) with Augie Pabst at the wheel. Also on the grid is Art Riley's Volvo P1800 (51), a Simca-Abarth (70) and John Everly (106), who bought the first customer Cobra racer in late 1962. Penske leads an interesting assortment of GT cars toward the first turn as practice begins, left. Seen here is the Volvo (51), John Everly's privateer Cobra (106), Mike Gammino's Ferrari 250 GTO (23), George Butler's Cobra (49), Bob Holbert's Cobra (98), and the Porsche 904s of Chuck Cassel (6) and Mike Kurkjian (54).

**Nassau, 1963**
An intent Roger Penske practicing for the Nassau Tourist Trophy, which he had won in record time the previous year. It was during this practice session, however, that some potentially expensive rod noises were heard from this car, which prompted its withdrawal from the race. The special Nassau hood is clearly visible here; the louvers were intended to improve cooling of the engine compartment. Also apparent here is the hood stripe (white on this car) which allowed the pit crew to easily identify the cars from the pits.

**Nassau, 1963**

Jim Hall at speed on the previous pages during practice for the Tourist Trophy. This was to be Hall's only appearance in the Grand Sport at Nassau since his main focus was on the performance of his new rear-engined Chaparral 2. Note the oil on the right rear fender, which was a sign of trouble to come. The number 65 car was marked with a black stripe. Veteran Grand Sport driver, Dr. Dick Thompson, is seen above in the number 80 car. Thompson was by far the most experienced driver of these cars, having been involved with them since the original Sebring brake test in December of 1962. Thompson had also driven the Grady Davis Grand Sport in a number of 1963 races prior to the car being returned to Chevrolet for modification. When asked about the differences between the old car and the Nassau car, Thompson replied, "The engine and the horsepower, also some of the aerodynamics, were much improved." The number 80 car was marked with a red stripe; note that the white number circles of the number 80 and number 50 cars were outlined in black, while the number circle on the number 65 car was not.

**Nassau, 1963**
When the Grand Sports were entrusted to the John Mecom Racing Team for Nassau in December of 1963, Mecom produced an impressive lineup of drivers to pilot these awesome machines. During a break in practice, from left, Augie Pabst, Roger Penske, Dick Thompson and Jim Hall enjoy a casual chat. All this and A. J. Foyt, too. Any other team of this era would have given anything for just one of these drivers—John Mecom had them all.

**Nassau, 1963**
Action in the five-lap qualifying race prior to the Tourist Trophy main event, above. Augie Pabst in the Lola coupe (00), Thompson (80) and Hall (65) charge through an S-curve. No other car in the qualifying race could begin to match the speed of these three, and Pabst won the race in record time with Hall and Thompson finishing second and third.

**Nassau, 1963**
John Mecom in the white sweater and Roger Penske in a Goodyear jacket talk to Dick Thompson prior to the start of the Nassau Trophy Race, left. Jim Hall, in the number 65 car, is in the background.

**Nassau, 1963**

A reverse angle of the front row for the start of the Nassau Trophy race shows a good view of the rare Lola coupe at pole position, right. This was the only Lola to get away from Ford, who was using it as a test vehicle for the forthcoming GT40. It was powered by a Traco-built Chevy 327 and was fast in the hands of veteran driver Augie Pabst. Motor racing journalist Bernard Cahier (with cap) is setting Pabst up for a prerace photograph.

**Nassau, 1963**

As the Nassau Trophy race is flagged off, Thompson takes the lead over Hall and Pabst, below. In the second rank are the Cobras of Butler (49), Everly (106) and Holbert (98). Gammino's 250 GTO (23) is close behind.

**Nassau, 1963**
By the time the cars reached the
bridge, Thompson, Hall and Pabst are
already pulling away from the Cobras
and the rest of the field.

**Nassau, 1963**

Rough track conditions as the cars pass under the bridge and into the first corner, at right. The Oakes Field course was full of holes and specialized in destroying suspensions. The surface was partly responsible for the poor showing of the Cobras, as their leaf spring suspensions just could not stand up to the beating of the poor surface. Thompson (80) still holds the lead with Hall (65), Pabst (00), Butler (49), Gammino (23) and Holbert (98) following up. Hall and Thompson ran this close, below, for the first nine laps, until Hall went out on the ninth lap—while in the lead—with an overheated rear axle. The Grand Sports were a full 11 seconds faster than the Cobras, and only the Lola could keep pace with them.

**Nassau, 1963**
The lead then passed to Dick Thompson, shown top left leading the Pabst Lola. The front-end lift of the Grand Sport is apparent here; it was never cured. On lap ten, above, Pabst turned up the power and took the lead for good. Here the Mecom Lola-Chevy pulls away from Dick Thompson's smoking Grand Sport, the rear end of which had given up, forcing Thompson to retire on lap 15. The race was stopped at the end of 22 laps due to darkness. The rear axle problem revealed a major flaw in the Grand Sport design, and much work would be done before the cars raced again on December 6 in the Governor's Cup race. The Grand Sports' rear differential was their Achilles heel, top right. The problem seemed to be that the Dana limited-slip differentials were green and not broken in. A frantic call to Detroit resulted in broken-in gears being hand-carried to Nassau. Oil coolers—adapted from production car automatic transmission coolers—were also ordered to help cool the rear-end lubricant. Note again the Firestone spare while the cars are running on Goodyears.

**Nassau, 1963**

After the Nassau Trophy race, the rear-end oil coolers were mounted on the cars. The system, as seen here, had a pump that pushed the oil from the differential, through a radiator mounted on the rear deck lid just behind the rear window and back. This new setup worked and the rear-end problem was solved. The coffee cup on the rear quarter panel testifies to the long hours put in by the mechanics to solve this problem. The exhaust pipe here on Penske's car has also seen some action. Also note the vacationing Chevrolet engineer, with Polaroid camera, checking out the front braking system.

**Nassau, 1963**
A close-up view at left of the newly installed oil radiator on the number 65 car. Note the sanitary installation of the cooler, right down to the matching paint. Par for the course on the Mecom team.

**Nassau, 1963**
Roger Penske (50) and Dick Thompson (80) lead the field in the early part of the first lap of the Nassau Governor's Cup race, below. Behind Penske can be seen the eventual winner, A. J. Foyt in the rear-engined Scarab (77), and Augie Pabst, making his only drive in a Grand Sport, car 003 (65).

**Nassau, 1963**
A hard-charging Roger Penske passes under the bridge on the start-finish straightaway during the running of the Governor's Cup race on December 6, 1963, below. Penske finished a creditable third, on the same lap as winner A. J. Foyt in the Mecom team Scarab. Second place went to Pedro Rodriguez in a factory Ferrari 250P prototype. Augie Pabst finished fourth and Dick Thompson, although not running at the finish, was scored sixth. The three Grand Sports had finished in the top ten while their Shelby adversaries were well back in the standings.

Canadian John Cannon, right, took over the wheel of Mecom Grand Sport 003 for the Nassau Trophy race. Cannon was first seen on the American racing scene in 1962 at the wheel of the brutal Canadian Dailu sports racer. He became a Mecom team driver and drove the Grand Sport at Nassau in 1963 and at Sebring in 1964.

## Nassau, 1963

On December 8, 1963, the entrants for the main event, the 252 mile Nassau Trophy race, were pushed into position for the running Le Mans start, above. The Mecom Scarab (77) of A. J. Foyt can be seen in the foreground. The Mecom crew is also pushing the 003 Grand Sport (65) of team newcomer John Cannon into position, while in the background, Cannon and Dick Thompson push Thompson's new Grand Sport 004 ride to its spot on the starting grid. Others on the grid are the Cooper Monaco (71), two Ferrari prototypes (85 and 90) and a works Austin-Healey (license number 54 FAC). The flag has dropped, the drivers have sprinted across the track, jumped into their cars and are starting their engines, right. As the cars pull out, the two Grand Sports are visible behind Penske's Cooper Chevy (36). From pole position are a Ferrari Testa Rossa with a Chevy V–8 (95), another Testa Rossa (85), Corvette Sting Ray (149), Cooper Monaco (16), Testa Rossa (22), the Mecom Scarab (77), Cooper Monaco (36) and the two Grand Sports. Down the line are a Jaguar E-Type, Ferrari GTO, Volkswagen Beetle and a Lancia Appia (37), with the Triumph TR4 (88) beating them all to the punch.

**Nassau, 1963**

Roger Penske, the race leader in the Cooper Chevy (36), laps the car he drove earlier in the week, top. The 004 number 50 Grand Sport was now being driven by Dick Thompson, running in third place. While Penske was lapping at record speed, Thompson, in the photo above, was pulling away from George Butler's Cobra (49), Chuck Cassel's Porsche (60) and Ray Heppenstall's Cooper-Ford (7).

**Nassau, 1963**

The Grand Sports of Dick Thompson and John Cannon are running in third and fourth place, top, again behind Foyt and Rodriguez's Ferrari.

A new problem is about to occur, however, as the air pressure is building up under the hoods and will soon cause the hood fasteners to come undone. This will cause both

cars to make a series of pit stops to have the hoods taped down. Running in fourth place, above, John Cannon laps John Everly's Cobra. Cannon, a charging Canadian driver, had never

set foot in the Grand Sport until he raced it in the Nassau Trophy. A pretty fair accomplishment under the circumstances.

**Nassau, 1963**
Dick Thompson signals trouble to John Cannon as he prepares to stop to have his hood taped down, above. The numerous pit stops dropped Thompson to fourth and Cannon to eighth in the final standings.

**Nassau, 1963**
Augie Pabst demonstrates his new found limbo stick skills to Bob Holbert at the Nassau victory party.

# Chapter 4

# Penske, Hall, Foyt and more

The success of Chevrolet's Nassau invasion was ample proof of the Grand Sports' mettle. Given sufficient horsepower and support, the Lightweights could be competitive against the Cobras. It was hardly surprising, then, that Knudsen and Arkus-Duntov set their sights on Daytona and Sebring.

Daytona's tri-oval had first been used for sports car racing as early as April 1959, when a USAC sports car race was held on the 2.5 mile high-speed circuit. Road racing activities were expanded in 1962, with the opening of an additional 1.3 mile infield road course for the three-hour Continental in February. For 1964, the length of the race was stretched to 2,000 kilometers, ranking it as the top endurance race in the country after Sebring. It was a perfect site to show off the Grand Sports' long-legged capabilities.

## Modifications to the modified

The elevated speeds permitted by Daytona's high banks prompted doubts about the coupes' competitiveness due to the effect of their prodigious frontal area on their top speed. Arkus-Duntov therefore decided to equip the two leftover Grand Sports—chassis numbers 001 and 002, still at the Chevrolet factory—with roadster bodies to reduce their frontal area and thus gain the highest possible top speed. (Interestingly, Shelby's designer, Pete Brock, had chosen an entirely different solution to the aerodynamic issue. By turning the Cobra roadster into the Daytona Coupe, he was able to increase its top speed dramatically.)

---

**"It was plumb-wild. After I let the clutch out, I knew the car would go. I just didn't know if it would stop."**
*Driver Delmo Johnson*

---

In addition to the 001 and 002 roadsters, the other three Grand Sport coupes received numerous updates prior to their planned assault on the two Florida tracks. Among the modifications were a new hood—designed to eliminate the lifting problems encountered at Nassau—and revised suspension trim. According to contemporary engineering records, in January 1964 the front and rear suspensions on Grand Sports 001, 004 and 005 were reworked with higher-rate springs. The paperwork suggests that 002 needed additional work to bring it into compliance with the others, which is consistent with the fact that 002 had never been seen outside of

Chevrolet. The 003 coupe, on the other hand, was noted as having already received the changes. Given the short lead time before Daytona, the work was conducted at a breakneck pace. "Please expedite!" read one request from early January. "Material should be available for installation by 1–20–64." A subsequent request stated a shipping deadline of January 31, the very eve of the February 16 Daytona race.

But it was all over even as it started; before the roadsters could be completed or the coupes fully modified, the corporate ax fell for good. Too much publicity concerning the Grand Sports had leaked out and the corporate heads of GM took Knudsen to task again, announcing that GM was in no way associated with the Mecom Racing Team. The insiders at Chevrolet responded by turning the three coupes over to privateers, delivering the cars with the same equipment as they carried at Nassau, including the Weber 58 DCOE carburetor set, but with 377 ci iron blocks in place of the original aluminum versions. As for the roadsters, they remained a well-kept secret within Warren.

With the dreams of Daytona snuffed out, the next major race of 1964 was Sebring, and all three coupes would be reunited there. In the meantime, the ex-Dick Doane 003 Grand Sport went to John Mecom, who sent it to his shop in Houston where it is believed to have remained until Sebring. The 005 car went to Jim Hall, who immediately shipped it to Roger Penske for Sebring preparation. "I really had no time for that car," said Hall. "I was too busy preparing the Chaparrals for the upcoming season so I sent the Grand Sport to Roger's shop in Pennsylvania. Roger's crew did all of the preparation on the car during the 1964 season and I only saw it when I co-drove it at the races."

## Texan versus Texan

The saga of the ex-Grady Davis 004 car is somewhat more controversial. Its story begins in early February, at the SCCA's annual convention, held that year in Dallas, Texas. Convention guest of honor was Carroll Shelby, who, after enduring ample praise for his exploits, announced that he would be bringing his Shelby American racing team to compete in Texas at the Convention Classic, held in conjunction with the meeting. And with that, a small regional race at the 1.9 mile Green Valley Raceway outside Fort Worth suddenly became big news with the imminent arrival of an A-Production Cobra and a prototype tube-frame Cooper King Cobra. The race became even bigger when Delmo Johnson, Jr., a seasoned SCCA racer and heir to Dallas' largest Chevrolet dealer-

**Sebring, March 1964**
A. J. Foyt and Roy Gane discuss the virtues of the Grand Sport's Italian carburetion system during pre-race preparation of the Mecom 003 Grand Sport.

ship, announced that he wanted to campaign one of the Mecom team Grand Sports (likely the 004 car) in *A-Production*.

As race organizers clamored to see how the two cars could be classed together, Shelby complained in *Sports Car* magazine: "I had to go to the bank and borrow money to build 100 Cobras so I could race against the Sting Rays. John Mecom is one of the richest young men in Texas. Let him build 100 of these cars and I'll run my production car against them."

Johnson, every bit the tough-talking Texan Shelby was, contended that the Grand Sport was just as eligible for the production classification as the Cobra: "This car is as much a production car as his racing version of the Cobras," he contested. "The only difference is his looks like a production car, ours doesn't. It is Chevrolet's answer to the racing Cobras—a racing Sting Ray."

By the time of race day, the burgeoning grudge match had attracted some 12,000 fans. But just as race officials had arranged for the Production and Modified cars to run together, Shelby withdrew his Production Cobra, pitting Johnson against Bob Holbert in the King Cobra. "I've got my modified car here," said Shelby. "They have theirs. Now let's have at it."

Unfortunately, the confrontation degraded into more sizzle than steak: Johnson's car made one practice lap—his first-ever lap behind the Grand Sport's wheel—before the clutch failed. Once it was repaired, Johnson had to go to the grid without any practice. "It was plumb-wild," he said. "After I let the clutch out, I knew the car would go. I just didn't know if it would stop."

As it happened, Shelby got at least partial revenge for his Nassau losses. Of the two races in which the two cars ran, the Corvette retired from both with overheating woes, giving the victory to Holbert.

**Road to Sebring**

Shortly after the Green Valley duel, Grady Davis apparently retrieved his Grand Sport and took it to the new three-mile Augusta International Speedway in Georgia for the season inaugural of the SCCA's United States Road Racing Championship on March 1. Its pilot in the fifty-two-lap event was famed Corvette driver Don Yenko, in what appears to have been his only Grand Sport ride. Once again, the King Cobras—driven by Dave MacDonald and Bob Holbert—were the leaders of the pack, and Yenko was relegated to eleventh overall behind George Wintersteen's Elva-Porsche.

---

**"When I first drove this vibrating, reverberating monster through the pits, I knew this feeling was completely unproduction-like."**
*Driver Ben Moore*

---

Meanwhile, Johnson had been bitten by the Grand Sport bug and arranged to buy the 004 car from Davis for $8,000. He immediately began preparations for Sebring, where his car would rejoin the other two coupes. There, the Grand Sports' main competition would come from the mid-engine Ferrari prototypes and the Cobras, the latter group trotting out a 427 ci engined Cobra roadster prototype, to be driven by Ken Miles. Both would present a daunting challenge for cars that really weren't prepared to take on factory-supported teams. But Johnson was buoyant about his car's chances: "Sebring is a twelve-hour race, period," he said. "You could just be spectacular—you could be a Stirling Moss for ten hours—but if you went out in the last two hours, then you'd sure wasted those ten hours." In practice, Johnson and co-driver Dan Morgan qualified twelfth behind the Dan Gurney/Bob Johnson Cobra roadster.

The Hall 005 Grand Sport was to be driven by Penske and Hall, and was beautifully prepared, painted Chaparral white with a broad blue stripe. In addition, it was fitted with an integral pneumatic jacking system that shortened pit stops. It was the sixth fastest qualifier behind four Ferrari prototypes and the Dave MacDonald/ Bob Holbert Cobra Daytona Coupe.

As for the Mecom team, most of its efforts had been directed toward Daytona, leaving just the Grand Sport and the Lola-Chevy for Sebring. Although impeccably finished on the outside, Mecom's Grand Sport 003 would never receive the attention it needed to survive the rigors of Sebring's half-day torment. Its drivers would be A. J. Foyt and John Cannon, but due to mechanical problems, Foyt failed to gain a spot on the grid and was classed sixty-second in a sixty-six car field. On the morning of the race, however, Foyt voiced confidence: "With all this horsepower," he said, "I really think I can outrun the Cobras with the lightweight Corvette."

At precisely 10:00 am on Saturday, March 21, 1964, starter Joe Lane gave the signal for the assembled drivers to scramble across the tarmac and into their cars. Penske was among the first off the mark, and he handily demonstrated what the Grand Sports did best: go fast in a straight line. By the end of the first lap, Penske had caught and passed all of the Ferrari prototypes on the back straight and was assuming the lead. As he passed the pits, he was even managing to pull away. But it was all over in the corners; while the Ferraris couldn't match the Corvette's power, they could always outcorner it.

Sebring 1964 was the first real test for the Grand Sports, and each team did its best to cope with the demands of the grueling race. "What a difference [from Nassau]!" wrote Steve Smith in *Car and Driver*. "Without Chevrolet's TLC, it was every man for himself."

At one point, Penske limped into the pits with a broken half-shaft. Because the Grand Sport's suspension was at least dimensionally similar to the production Corvette, Hall and Penske were able to "borrow" a halfshaft from a spectator's Corvette in the paddock, install it on the Grand Sport, and get back in the race. A note was left on the spectator's windshield explaining why his car had been pirated. When asked recently about this incident, Penske smiled and said, "Sometimes you have to do anything to stay in the race."

The Foyt/Cannon 003 car was less fortunate. Although it had run in the top ten for nine hours and was at one point as high as eighth overall, it was sidelined during the ninth hour of the race when worn splines caused it to lose a wheel. In keeping with Sebring rules, Cannon brought a spare back out to the car and managed to get the car back to the pits. Just as the repaired car was speeding down pit lane in the dark of night, Consalvo Sanesi, in his flagging and dimly illuminated Alfa Romeo TZ 1, was hugging the pit wall, ostensibly out of harm's way. But closing in fast behind—and unable to see the Alfa—was Bob Johnson in the Gurney Cobra. As the two cars collided in a fiery crash, Cobra crewman Tony Storr was rushing across the pit road to the accident scene and was hit by the exiting Cannon. According to Steve Smith, "Storr was thrown so far and so high that many witnesses thought Sanesi had tumbled out of the Alfa when it was fifteen feet airborned." Fortunately, Storr was not seriously injured, while the Alfa burned throughout the night.

In the end, the Grand Sports' Sebring results were not that far off the mark, considering the cars they were racing against. And given that there were only a total of four cars running in their class at the finish—Miles' seven-liter Cobra had retired with engine failure just ten minutes before the end of the race—the results had to look good. Indicative of the car's sheer speed—as well as Penske's outstanding talent—was a near-record lap time for the 005 car. On his sixth lap, Penske turned the 5.2 mile course in 3:12.2, less than a second behind John Surtees' 1963 lap record of 3:11.4 in a SEFAC Ferrari 250P. Penske's preparation paid off with first in class honors, eighteenth overall behind Ed Leslie's MGB. Foyt and Cannon's 003, after falling as low as twenty-seventh overall, finished twenty-third, second in class. The Johnson 004 car, with its proud owner and Dave Morgan driving, took thirty-second.

The rest of the summer was a quiet one for Chevrolet's secret sports cars. Although Mecom's 005 car appears to have been dormant, Hall's car came in handy as a backup entry for that year's Road America in September when one of his Chaparrals was not ready in time. The car was driven by Roger Penske, Jim Hall and Hap Sharp, who alternated driving assignments between the Chaparral and the Grand Sport. Penske, who always did well at Road America, recalled that it "was a great track for the Grand Sport, you could use all of the power and hit 175 mph on the long straight."

Penske started the race and worked his way up to the top four. From there on, it was a classic duel between the Grand Sport, Miles' 289 Cobra and a John Mecom Ferrari 250LM driven by Augie Pabst and Walt Hansgen. Penske diced it out with the Ferrari for first, eventually surrendering, but continuing a ferocious fight with Miles for second. As with the Mecom Grand Sport at Sebring, wheel problems struck again, consigning Penske to third place behind the Ferrari and Cobra.

**Mexican Carrera**

Johnson continued to campaign his 004 car in a variety of Southwestern events, including a little-known attempt to revive the Mexican Road Race in late 1964. Called the Carrera de Costa a Costa, this staged time-distance race ran from Veracruz on the eastern coast to Acapulco on the western coast, with intermediate stops in Puebla, Mexico City, Cuernavaca, Taxco and Chilpancingo. Unlike the original race, however, this event was relatively loosely organized—with concomitant results to spectator and participant alike.

Johnson's car was trucked to Mexico City before traveling east to Veracruz. Johnson, along with a Mexican translator provided for

the trip by the Pemex Oil Company, decided to drive the car there himself rather than trailering it: "After we pulled into Mexico City, we unloaded the car. I wanted to put a couple of miles on the engine, so we decided to go to Veracruz on the highway." At one point, Johnson remembered, the car was traveling in excess of 150 mph, when it met some unexpected company. "We came around a corner and there were some motorcycle cops. The translator told me, 'They're either going to put us in prison or let us go by.' They pulled off their hats and waved us on."

---

*"I realized how fast I was closing on other cars and jumped on the brakes. It was like a huge hand reached out and gave me instant deceleration and I missed a calamity by a scant six inches."*
*Driver Ben Moore*

---

As Johnson and his passenger neared Veracruz, they were detoured off the road, with disastrous results. "The Grand Sport was very low to the ground," said Johnson, "with about 3½ inches of ground clearance. During the detour, we knocked the oil filter off, but we didn't have any spares with us—they were all with the truck back in Mexico City. The best we could do was to persuade the driver of an old Chevy taxicab to sell us the filter off his car and hope that we would make it."

As they neared Veracruz, a rear axle oil cooler line was knocked off, causing the ring and pinion to, in Johnson's words, "weld themselves together." Johnson and the translator then abandoned the Grand Sport and hitchhiked to Veracruz, leaving the car for the support truck to rescue. After finding a pleasant local saloon in which to pass the time, Johnson was eventually tracked down by his mechanic Bill Goodfellow.

"Goodfellow," asked Johnson, "how did you find me?"

"Simple," he responded, "this was the first bar in town. Where else would you expect me to find you?"

Now, all of this had taken place before the race had even got underway. With the arrival of the rescue truck, the rear end was repaired and Johnson was staged to depart at 12:15 pm the following day with the next car to follow a minute later. As Johnson recalled, the car after his went into the crowds, killing or injuring eleven people.

In order to go as far as possible between staging areas, the Johnson car was carrying fifty-five gallons of fuel in a steel drum mounted in place of the normal fiberglass tank. Unfortunately, Johnson was traveling so fast that his crew couldn't keep up. "In order to keep going, I'd pull into a filling station and bargain for fuel. In order to keep the octane up, I used some stuff called Horsepower in a Can."

The road surface, as Johnson recalled, was hardly suitable for any race car, let alone a handbuilt prototype with barely four inches of ground clearance. "We were bouncing down a Mexican highway that looked like washboard. The frame was hitting the ground every thirty feet, and actually wore through some of the tubes." By the time they got to Acapulco, said Johnson with a certain degree of understatement, the car "needed a lot of work."

After it returned to Dallas, Johnson's car served primarily as an attention getter, especially when it was run on the street. In late 1964 or early 1965, he sold it to Canadian David Greenblatt for $8,000, a sum so high for a "wore-out" car that Johnson "laughed for a year."

He no longer finds it quite so funny.

## Return to Nassau

In October 1964, the Hall 005 car made one of its last appearances as Roger Penske loaned it to veteran Corvette driver Ben Moore for an SCCA regional race in Reading, Pennsylvania. Penske had originally contacted Moore to see if he might be interested in buying the car: "I couldn't believe my ears when he offered to let me try the car out at the upcoming Reading road races," said Moore recently. "Of course the understanding was, you wreck it, you bought it. Previous to the Reading races, I had never run a single lap in a modified car of any kind."

Moore, like many before him, was quick to appreciate the Grand Sport's awesome horsepower. "From the moment I sat myself into that functional, austere cockpit," he recalled, "the feeling was that here was an all-out racing machine that was indeed noteworthy. This car was a dream come true for me. When I first drove this vibrating, reverberating monster through the pits, I knew this feeling was completely unproduction-like. When the green flag dropped, I let the clutch out and the car almost stalled, then with a breathtaking lurch, the Grand Sport was underway.

"On the first lap, I must have passed five or six cars. As I came to one of the 180 degree turns, I realized how fast I was closing on other cars and jumped on the brakes. It was like a huge hand reached out and gave me instant deceleration and I missed a calamity by a scant six inches. Fantastic brakes and frightening acceleration, this car had it all.

"This experience turned me on to the real potential of this car and I won the race with a first overall and a first in the C-Modified class. This had to be the most exciting, if not the most important, day of my short racing career. Even the feeling of the high banks at Daytona (which scared the daylights out of me) could never surpass this one. I feel extremely fortunate to have had this experience, and extremely stupid for not having purchased that car from Roger."

After the Road America race—but before the car was turned over to Moore—the Grand Sport was brought back to Penske's shop, where it was readied for Nassau. Penske remembers that Bill Scott "was responsible for preparing the car for Nassau. He did a complete rebuild of the car and we had everything magnafluxed. The engine was sent to Traco and completely rebuilt. [In a post-race interview with *Corvette News,* Penske described it as a destroked, iron-block 377 ci engine.] We also replaced the wheel bearings and knock-off spinners; we had found that these were worn and that was why we had wheel problems at Road America. To lighten the car, the jacking and water pressure systems were removed." When it was complete, the car weighed in at about 1,900 pounds, some 300 pounds less than normal.

At Nassau, the Hall/Penske 005 car would be joined by the Mecom 003 Grand Sport. Driving for the Mecom team would be stock car veteran Jack Saunders.

The first Nassau event was the Tourist Trophy race, preceded as usual by a five-lap qualifier that often proved to be as exciting as the race itself. This year, after seeing Chevrolet walk away with all the spoils in 1963, Carroll Shelby had prepared an extra-potent Cobra prototype powered by an aluminum-block 390 ci experimental engine to be driven by Ken Miles. It made an immediate impression on Roger Penske: "I learned something during the five-lap race that was very important. I knew that I could never compete with that monster of Ken's on the straights, so that if I were to win, I'd have to take him in the corners." And that was saying something for a car known more for its power on the straights than its calm in the corners.

It hardly mattered, however, for Shelby's aluminum engine failed early in the race. With the monster Cobra out of the way, the only thing Penske had to confront was Mother Nature. Late in the afternoon, the skies opened, turning the recently repaved race course into an oil-slick skating rink. "When the big rainstorm dropped," Penske told *Corvette News,* "I had to slow to 30 or 35 miles per hour for the last two laps . . . It was so slippery that I would lose wheel traction every time I took my foot off the gas. You see, the engine drag slowed the wheel rotation to a point where the wheels couldn't rotate as fast as the car was moving forward because they couldn't grip the road." But the front-end lift during acceleration, added Penske, caused the front tires to lose their bite, turning the car into a huge, plowing mass. Nonetheless, Penske prevailed and won the event, giving him the first win in a Nassau hat trick along with a record lap speed of 93.03 mph.

Sometime during the week between the Tourist Trophy race and the Governor's Cup race that followed it, the Hall/Penske Grand Sport was sold to gentleman racer George Wintersteen, an old friend of Penske. Wintersteen's ex-Penske Cooper-Chevy (which was a replacement for his Elva-Porsche) had been damaged in a crash at Laguna Seca earlier in the year and resisted Wintersteen's best efforts to get it sorted out for Nassau. "My Cooper wasn't running very well," he recalled, "so a friend of mine—Peter Goetz—and I approached Roger with the idea of buying the car to run at Sebring in 1965. The deal was completed and I drove the Grand Sport for the rest of the Nassau events."

During the 100 mile Governor's Cup on the Friday preceding the Nassau Trophy finale on Sunday, neither of the Grand Sports finished. Jack Saunders in 003 dropped out on the twenty-second lap of the twenty-five-lap event, while Wintersteen completed only twelve laps before succumbing to mechanical problems.

At the main event, the 250 mile Nassau Trophy race, rain was again everyone's nemesis. Wintersteen's was the lone Grand Sport, as the Mecom Corvette had failed to gain a place on the grid. The drenched Oakes Field track seemed to send everyone spinning; Hugh Dibley's Brabham was taken out by a Sunbeam Alpine, A. J. Foyt went off-course in the Hussein-Dodge, Penske spun the Chaparral 2 and Phil Hill left the circuit not realizing that he had done so.

Wintersteen did his best to cope with the Corvette's treacherous handling in the wet, but *Autocar* noted that he, too, had his off-course excursions: "the new owner [of Penske's Grand Sport] wasn't quite a match for the prodigious power in the wet, with the result that the bodywork was considerably modified with each successive shunt. 'Take a look at the Lightweight!' chanted one of Penske's mechanics, 'It's getting lighter every lap!'"

But if George Wintersteen and the others thought that the Oakes Field course was tough in the rain, they were in for something of a surprise at Sebring the following March.

**Green Valley, Texas, February 1964**
Bob Holbert's Shelby King Corbra (98) leads Alan Connell's Cooper Monaco (47) and others. Delmo Johnson and the 004 Grand Sport are in sixth place; the car was never a challenger and suffered clutch and cooling problems. Holbert went on to win.

Once the largest Chevrolet dealer in Dallas, Delmo Johnson earned a solid reputation in SCCA racing driving solid-axle Corvettes, above. He purchased the 004 Grand Sport from John Mecom in early 1964 and campaigned it in 1964 with longtime friend Dave Morgan. Johnson is shown here at right sharing some Texas laughs with Jim Hall. *Bill Neale*

**Augusta, Georgia, March 1964**
The Grady Davis 004 Grand Sport at the inaugural USRRC on March 1, 1964, at the Augusta International Speedway, right. Two Cheetahs rest in the background.

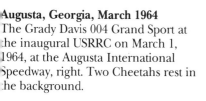

**Augusta, Georgia, March 1964**
Action from the Augusta race, above.
Driver Don Yenko finished eleventh
overall in his sole Grand Sport ride.

**Sebring, March 1964**
Roger Penske takes a cameraman for
a ride around the Sebring course
during practice, left. The car still
wears most of its modified equipment
from Nassau although the hood
scoops have been taped shut.

**Sebring, March 1964**
Two hard chargers running together, above. Roger Penske in the Hall/Penske 005 Grand Sport leads A. J. Foyt in the Mecom 003 car away from the MG bridge in the early hours of the 12-hour duel. The infamous Grand Sport front-end lift is obvious here on Penske's mount as he accelerates out of the chicane. Another Texas entry at Sebring in 1964 was the Grand Sport 004 of Johnson Chevrolet, Dallas, left. Driven by Delmo Johnson and Dave Morgan, the car suffered continuous mechanical woes, finally finishing thirty-second overall.

**Sebring, March 1964**
Into the night, the Mecom team 003
Grand Sport pits for a tire change.

**Nassau, December 1964**
The John Mecom Racing Team returned to Nassau in 1964, left, in an attempt to repeat their wins of 1963 over Shelby's Cobras. Mecom and crew, including driver Jack Saunders in the funny hat, push Grand Sport 003 from the quay. Mecom is at the rear of the car. The hangar that served as a giant garage during the Nassau Speed Week, below. Mecom's lineup of cars is evident, with the Grand Sport 003 in the center.

**Watkins Glen, June 1966**
The Grand Sports' last gasp in the form of the two roadsters, 001 and 002. George Wintersteen raced 002, here, with moderate success in the USRRC series of 1966. He piloted the car well but was outclassed by the mid-engined McLarens and Lolas.

**Sebring, March 1966**
The Penske 001 Grand Sport roadster in the Sebring garage during prerace preparation. Note the fine detail work of Penske's team: even the side exhaust pipes are painted yellow as part of the car's colors. Dick Guldstrand is at work under the hood with George Wintersteen peering over his shoulder and Bill Scott smiling for the camera. *Norman Ahn*

A line-up of the famous Corvette racers, gathered together at the 1985 Bloomington Gold Corvette show in Bloomington, Illinois. In the front row are the four restored Grand Sports. From left: roadster 001, at the time owned by Jim Purvis of Overland Park, Kansas; coupe 004, owned by Jamey Mazzotta of Redding, California; coupe 003, owned by Bob Paterson of Woodside, California; and roadster 002, owned by Ed Mueller of Hawthorne, New Jersey. In the background is the Corvette SS and the Bill Mitchell Sting Ray racer built on the SS Mule chassis. *Marilyn Purvis*

**Grand Sport roadster 001**
Owned by Gene Schiavone of Essex, Connecticut. Restored by former owner Jim Purvis to Roger Penske's colors as of Sebring 1966. Schiavone expects to campaign the car in vintage racing events. *Marilyn Purvis*

**Grand Sport roadster 002**
Owned by Ed Mueller of Hawthorne, New Jersey. The car is restored as of 1989 to the same trim as when it was last raced by George Wintersteen in 1966. Before being sold to Mueller, the car was only seen twice in public in 21 years. The cockpit of the roadster, right, spare yet immaculately restored.

**Grand Sport coupe 003**
Owned by Bob Paterson of Woodside, California. After being raced by Dick Doane, John Mecom and Alan Sevadjian, and driven by Augie Pabst, Jim Hall and John Cannon, the car made its way to Paterson in 1973. It has been restored as of 1989 to its Sebring 1964 colors. Paterson has campaigned the car for several years on the vintage racing circuit. *Maggie Logan*

**Grand Sport coupe 004**
Owned by Jamey Mazzotta of
Redding, California, above. After a
race career in the hands of Grady
Davis, John Mecom, Roger Penske,
Delmo Johnson, David Greenblatt and
Jim White Chevrolet, Mazzotta has
restored the car as of 1989 to its 1963
Nassau Speed Week garb. The only
difference in trim is the shade of blue
now on the car. Mazzotta has also
campaigned the car in vintage racing
events. *Maggie Logan*

**Grand Sport coupe 005**
Owned by Bill Tower of Plant City,
Florida, right. After racing with John
Mecom, Dick Thompson, Jim Hall,
Roger Penske and George
Wintersteen, the car is unrestored as
of 1989. The body and interior have
been stripped and the engine
removed.

**Sebring, March 1964**
Two of racing's most brilliant minds confer. Roger Penske, left, and Jim Hall engrossed in conversation concerning the Grand Sport's performance.

**Sebring, March 1964**
Jim Hall in Grand Sport 005 during practice for the Sebring race, below. This car was beautifully prepared; painted Chaparral white with blue trim, it was the fifth fastest qualifier for the race behind four prototype Ferraris and the Cobra Daytona coupe.

**Sebring, March 1964**
The rear pneumatic jack on car 005 is plainly visible here, to the rear of the differential. Also visible are the modifications made by the crew to the differential oil cooler. The large cooler in the center of the rear deck has been removed and two coolers, one on each fender, have been added.

**Sebring, March 1964**
The Hall/Penske 005 Grand Sport awaiting action, right. The two smaller differential oil coolers are visible here without air scoops covering them; the bolt holes from the old single cooler are unfilled at center. Also note the eight holes cut in the tail in line with the brakelights to aid airflow and cooling for the rear brakes and differential.

**Sebring, March 1964**
Jim Hall on the Warehouse Straight during practice, below. The small scoops for the differential oil coolers behind the rear window were removed before the race. The fittings on the front fender served the pneumatic jacks, left, and the engine cooling system, right. Note also the new gas filler cap and the running lights on either side of the number plate for night racing.

95

**Sebring, March 1964**
The engine mounted in the 005 Grand Sport at Sebring was the same 377 ci, 485 hp model that appeared at Nassau. The only difference was that the engine block was cast iron rather than aluminum. The monstrous 58 mm DCOE Webers are still prominent.

## Sebring, March 1964

The oil cooler setup, above, on the Delmo Johnson 004 Grand Sport; the Mecom 003 car had the same setup. Also seen are the ducts in the top of the plexiglass rear window used for cooling the brakes and the rear end. As the tires got wider, so did the fenders, right. This fender extension is not very neat, but it passed the technical inspection. Note the deep-dish Halibrand wheel. The car is back on Firestones, sized at 8.00/8.20 –15 at rear. The side exhaust pipe has changed from a bolt-mounting to a spring. The new Grand Sport hoods as they appeared at Sebring, here on 005, above right. Note the all-new venting system. The louvers in front are for venting warm air away from the radiator, while the louvers on the side panels are for pulling fresh air into the Weber carburetors. To keep the hoods down, leather straps and a shock cord fastener have been added. All three cars were equipped with the simple shock cord device.

**Sebring, March 1964**
The Jim Hall garage at Sebring. The Grand Sport in the background is undergoing the kind of race preparation that one would expect of this crew. In the foreground is the Porsche 904, co-driven by Chaparral regulars Hap Sharp and Ronnie Hissom. Hall remembers that the 904 "was a last-minute decision, since we had originally intended to run the Chaparrals, but rule changes prevented this." The 904 failed to finish.

**Sebring, March 1964**
Even the best engineering minds sometimes must consult their notes. Jim Hall, above, is caught checking his book of tricks during an engine rebuild on the 005 Grand Sport. A. J. Foyt adds a little of his mechanical expertise to the engine of the Mecom 003 entry, right, while Delmo Johnson, above right, plays photographer during some of the Sebring support races. Johnson was the twelfth fastest qualifier among an especially large field of cars.

**Sebring, March 1964**

"With all this horsepower," said A. J. Foyt on the morning of the race, above left, "I really think I can outrun the Cobras with the lightweight Corvette." Because of problems, Foyt did not receive a qualifying time and had to start in the sixty-second position. His work was cut out for him. Roger Penske, left, was equally confident about the competition. "To be honest with you," he told an interviewer, "we really want to blow the Cobras off." Penske would start in the sixth position, with only four Ferrari prototypes and the Cobra Daytona coupe in front of him. Penske was also a master of the Le Mans start. Jim Hall, above, felt that "we will give them a run for their money, and hope it all stays together."

**Sebring, March 1964**
The thrill of the Le Mans start! Ludovico Scarfiotti in the SEFAC Ferrari 275P (23) was first off the line, followed by the NART Ferrari 330P of Pedro Rodriguez (25) and Penske in the white Grand Sport 005 (4). Just coming off the line is John Surtees in the SEFAC Ferrari 330P (21) next to Graham Hill in the Maranello Concessionnaires 330P (24) followed by Mike Parkes's SEFAC 275P (22). Further down the line is Shaw in a Cobra (17) and a white and red Iso-Bizzarrini Grifo A3 Corsa off to a flying start.

## Sebring, March 1964

The cars race past the pits, above, with Penske's Grand Sport leading this pack, trailed by Shaw's Cobra, Bob Holbert in the Shelby Cobra Daytona coupe (10), Gurney in another Cobra (11) and Graham Hill's Ferrari 330P (24) off to a slow start. As the field moves off under the Mercedes Bridge, right, Scarfiotti lengthens his early lead and checks his rearview mirror for followers. Rodriguez (25) and Surtees (21) are close behind with Penske's Grand Sport accelerating hard, its front end flying high. Bob Holbert is still struggling to get the driver's door shut on his Daytona coupe. In the background is a Ferrari 250LM (28), the Guichet/Abate 1964 250 GTO (31), the Thompson/Grossman NART 250 GTO (29), the Stirling Moss team bright green SMART Lotus Elan (57) and various Alpines, Porsches and Alfa TZs. Roger Penske gave the huge crowd a vivid demonstration of the Grand Sport's capabilities, above right. On the back straight, he caught up with—and passed—all of the Ferrari prototypes to take the lead. Passing the pits at full speed, he was still pulling away. The Ferraris could catch him in the corners, but could not match his speed on the long straights. Scarfiotti is still on his tail but several lengths behind.

**Sebring, March 1964**
By lap three, top, Surtees (21) has passed, and looks in his mirror to see Penske wave Rodriguez (25) by. During the first hour, the only cars to pass the Grand Sport were the four Ferrari prototypes. While Penske was challenging the leaders, Delmo Johnson in car 004 was working his way up the ladder after a poor start, above left. Johnson has just passed the Hudson/Grant Corvette; looming in the background is A. J. Foyt's 003 Grand Sport. As Johnson approaches the first corner, Foyt and Hudson are hard on his heels, above right. When asked to describe the Grand Sport, Delmo Johnson said, "Brute horsepower. It was like a dragster—the only car I ever drove that would lift the front wheels off the ground in all four gears."

## Sebring, March 1964

Penske under full acceleration on the pit straight, left. His memories parallel Johnson's: "The Grand Sport was a very good car; one of its main attributes was its tremendous horsepower. It was so light in the front end that when you really stood on the gas, the front end would come off the ground like a dragster." A. J. Foyt slides the Mecom 003 Grand Sport through The Hairpin, below. After starting in sixty-second position, Foyt made one of the greatest first lap performances in Sebring history. He passed 50 cars *in the first lap*. Said Johnson of Foyt's talents: "No one ever drove harder than he did." Note the running lights on the roof and door number plate for night racing.

**Sebring, March 1964**
Continuing his charge to the front, right, Foyt leads the 427 prototype Cobra of Ken Miles (1) and the Cobra of French champion Jo Schlesser (14). Still running in the top five, below, Penske leads Mike Parkes' Ferrari 275P and a reconfigured Porsche 904 through the Webster Turns.

**Sebring, March 1964**
Ken Miles, in the thundering Cobra 427 prototype, leads Foyt's Grand Sport. These two ran together for quite awhile and constantly swapped places until the brakes in the big Cobra failed. The Grand Sport was originally built as the Cobra fighter, forcing Shelby to rebuke with this, his Corvette fighter.

**Sebring, March 1964**

A great American champion leads two European legends: A. J. Foyt holds off the Ferraris of John Surtees (21) and Graham Hill (24) through the Webster Turns, top left. A change of drivers and Jim Hall is at full speed on the Warehouse Straight in 005, above. Hall and Delmo Johnson running side-by-side down the Warehouse Straight ahead of Tommy Hitchcock's Cobra, top right. Note the whip antenna on the top of Johnson's car; he was one of the first to use radio communications with his pit. Obviously he had needed it considering the body damage to his Grand Sport.

**Sebring, March 1964**
John Cannon, now driving the Mecom car, slides through the Webster Turns.

**Sebring, March 1964**
Penske uses all of the available road on the fast left-hand sweeper at the end of the Start/Finish Straight. Note Sebring's famous heatwaves; the weather was hot and humid.

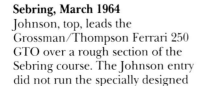

**Sebring, March 1964**
Johnson, top, leads the Grossman/Thompson Ferrari 250 GTO over a rough section of the Sebring course. The Johnson entry did not run the specially designed fiberglass Chevrolet headlight covers but stuck with the earlier plexiglass shields. A white Volvo P1800 and another Corvette bring up the rear. Penske comes into the pits with problems, above left. He had been running in the top six overall for the first six hours; only the five Ferrari prototypes were ahead. A halfshaft has broken and no spare is available, above right.

**Sebring, March 1964**
Penske to Hall, above: "There's a Corvette parked behind our pit and I bet we could borrow the halfshaft and leave the owner a note." Hall to Penske: "Lets do it." They did, and were back in the race one hour later. The Hall/Penske car passes the parked Johnson/Morgan car at The Hairpin, above right. Dave Morgan exits to check on one of the many problems encountered by this team during the 12 hour event. The lack of factory support was beginning to take its toll. The Johnson/Morgan Grand Sport during one of its many pit stops, right. Note the race tire tread.

**Sebring, March 1964**
The Johnson/Morgan Grand Sport shows its late-hour battle scars on the rear deck, top. Here is another good look at the whip antenna used for radio communication with the pits. Johnson recalled that the "crossover Webers were a beautiful system—they put out a tremendous amount of horsepower and were extremely responsive." Hall through the Webster Turns in late afternoon, above. Note that the headlight covers have now been removed.

**Sebring, March 1964**
The Johnson/Morgan car through the Webster Turns at dusk, top left. "When you went down the straight," said Johnson of his Grand Sport, "the car would jump from side to side. It

never did steer straight, but it always got you from corner to corner. I've never known exactly how it did it . . . As far as I'm concerned, if any driver ever says he had complete control of that car, he's lying to you." Jim Hall,

top right, is a study of concentration as he rounds The Hairpin at dusk. One can see the battle scars left from almost 12 hours of racing on a rough course. John Cannon exits The Hairpin at dusk, above. This car ran

in the top ten for nine hours and was as high as eighth overall. A broken wheel in the last hour dropped the Mecom entry to twenty-third overall at the finish.

**Sebring, March 1964**
Dave Morgan manages to smile as he exits his car for the last time during the final pit stop of a long day.

**Sebring, March 1964**
The Johnson/Morgan Grand Sport sits in the pits. The effect of a difficult day shows on the back body panels. This car suffered from various problems almost from the beginning, but still managed to finish thirty-second overall. It is a credit to the drivers and the teams that all three Grand Sports finished the race at all, due to the lack of spare parts and factory support.

**Road America, September 1964**

The next major appearance for the Grand Sport was at the Road America 500 in September 1964, above, where it became a last minute replacement for a second Jim Hall Chaparral that was not ready. The 005 car was driven by Roger Penske, Hall and Hap Sharp, who alternated driving assignments between the Chaparral and the Grand Sport. "We kind of left the officials scratching their heads about that one," said Hall. Penske, who always did well at Road America, started the race and worked his way up to the top four. He is seen here in the Thunder Valley section of the beautiful Road America circuit. Hap Sharp, top left, was once described by Jim Hall as "a man of a thousand ideas," and he proved to be a great asset to the successful Chaparral racing program. His only appearance in the Grand Sport was at Road America in September 1964 when he co-drove with Penske and Hall. Penske, top right, takes the inside line to pass a Maserati during the Road America 500. Meanwhile, the Chaparral was forced to retire with brake trouble while leading the race. Penske enters the pits for a routine stop, above right. Note the new hood—again. The louvers are gone and the bulge has been reduced.

**Road America, September 1964**
As Penske comes to a stop and undoes his harness, top, the pneumatic jack hose is attached and the refueling process begins. Penske exits the car, and the crew goes to work fueling, checking the oil and reading the tire temperatures, left.

**Road America, September 1964**
The left front wheel is changed, the
knock-off hub screwed back on and
tapped with a hammer for tightness. A
crewman with a fire extinguisher
watches from the tail of the car.

**Road America, September 1964**
The jack hose is unplugged and the car settles back onto its wheels, right. Jim Hall confers briefly with Hap Sharp before he roars back into the race. Sharp takes his turn at the wheel and passes Doug Revson's Elva-BMW along the way, below. This was Sharp's only appearance in a Grand Sport Corvette.

**Road America, September 1964**
Jim Hall, above, overtakes the Porsche RS of George Dickson while running in second place to the Mecom Ferrari 250LM. Roger Penske gives pit signals to Hall between driving stints, left. Even when he was driving, Penske was involved in the other aspects of the team effort. Jim Hall, far left, leads the Mecom Ferrari 250LM driven by Pabst and Hansgen. These two engaged in a furious duel for the lead, until the Ferrari took over for good.

**Road America, September 1964**
After surrendering the lead to the Ferrari, Hall began dueling with Ken Miles' Cobra for second place, top. These two swapped positions for the rest of the race. Note the tighter line

the Cobra follows through the turn while the Grand Sport rolls far and wide to the outside. Hall accelerates out of a left-hander and is chased by the ever present Miles, above left. Wuesthoff's Elva-Porsche (79), Bud

Gates' Genie (28) and O. J. Klein's Maserati (77) bring up the rear. Jim Hall comes in for the final pit stop, above right. Hall makes his exit from the car as the crew goes to work. Note

the smashed windshield from a flying stone thrown up by the rear wheel of another competitor. The left headlamp cover is also missing.

**Reading, Pennsylvania, October 1964**
In October 1964, above, Roger Penske loaned the 005 Grand Sport to veteran driver Ben Moore to drive at the SCCA Regional race at Reading. Moore won the race, finishing first overall and first in the C-Modified class.

**Carrera de Costa a Costa, Mexico, 1964**
Delmo Johnson's battered 004 Grand Sport upon its return from the Carrera revival race, left. Note the homemade cow catcher mounted on the front of the car. The number 1215 was also the car's departure time from the starting line. This is the sole photo (sadly out of focus) uncovered from the car's Mexican adventure. *Bill Neale*

**Nassau, December 1964**
John Mecom has the local police officer scratching his head with his request.

In August of 1964, above, Carroll Shelby and Ken Miles decided to build a special Cobra to take to Nassau and demolish the Corvette Grand Sports. The car had a lightened frame, a thin-gauge aluminum body and a special NASCAR experimental 390 ci aluminum engine. The car weighed barely 1,600 pounds and put out almost 500 hp. During tests, the car accelerated like a rocket but was extremely short on reliability. Only Miles could tame this beast.

**Nassau, December 1964**
The 003 Grand Sport returned to Nassau in late November 1964, right. John Mecom brought his large stable of cars to Nassau to see if he could repeat his 1963 victories. Jack Saunders, a relatively unknown driver, was to drive the Mecom Grand Sport this time. Saunders is on the right here, complete with funny hat, helping to push the car.

**Nassau, December 1964**
Two semi-interested tourists watch the Grand Sport move away from the dock toward the hangar that will serve as home for the next week of racing, left. Note the sideview mirror and the "Prepared by" logo on the door, waiting to be filled in. The differential oil cooler is back on the rear deck lid. The Mecom mechanics are hard at work preparing the cars for the first practice session, below. Also present in the hangar are a batch of Porsches and Coopers, Mecom's Zerex Special, a Cobra (76) and a VW Beetle (9).

**Nassau, December 1964**
The 1964 Mecom entry at Nassau, left, was a rather imposing sight: Mecom's Ferrari 250LM on wire wheels (3), Grand Sport 003 and several Zerex cars. The NART Ferrari 250 GTO (70) is parked down the line. Jack Saunders, above, leans on the fender of the Grand Sport he would drive in the Nassau Tourist Trophy. Saunders was an unknown driver by international standards when he appeared at Nassau; little is known of his racing career except that he competed in some SCCA events in the Texas area.

**Nassau, December 1964**
In the photo above, John Mecom, center, and some of his crew take time out at Nassau. Carroll Shelby in funny hat, John Mecom, center, and Hap Sharp are caught swapping some big Texas lies, above right. The Challenged: Ken Miles tests his 390 ci Cobra during practice, right.

## Nassau, December 1964

The Challenged: Jack Saunders getting some track time during practice for the Nassau Tourist Trophy, top left. The Challenged: Roger Penske in his extra-light 005 Grand Sport, top right. After the Road America race, the Grand Sport was brought back to the Penske shop in Newtown Square, Pennsylvania, where it was completely rebuilt in preparation for Nassau. To lighten the car, the jacking and water pressure systems were removed, bringing the weight down to about 1,900 pounds, a reduction of some 300 pounds. Note the patch over the former jack hose hole on the left fender. The start of the Nassau Trophy race shows Miles, Saunders and Penske in the front row, above. Earlier in the day, Penske had beaten Miles in the five-lap qualifying race. Bringing up the field is Phil Hill in the early Ford GT40 (91), the Mecom Ferrari 250LM (3) and a host of Volvos, Mustangs, Abarths, Sunbeams and a Renault Dauphine.

125

**Nassau, December 1964**
As the cars move under the bridge, right, Miles, Saunders and Penske are already pulling away from a respectable field that included Hill's Ford GT40 (91), Noseda's Cobra (103), Johnson's Cobra (92), Payne's Cobra (13) and Hansgen in the Ferrari 250LM (3). The Sunbeam Tiger (74) is keeping pace. Into the first lap, below, Miles leads Saunders, Penske, Hill and Hansgen.

**Nassau, December 1964**
At the end of the first lap, the brutal horsepower of Miles' Cobra is evident as he pulls out to a tremendous lead over the Grand Sports, in the far background.

**Nassau, December 1964**
Saunders and Penske pass under the bridge, above, leaving Phil Hill's Ford GT40 behind.

**Nassau, December 1964**
Jack Saunders leads Roger Penske, top. The two Grand Sports ran this close for several laps. It was the Clash of the Titans, above, two of the best drivers of the time, matched in equal cars—what could be better? Penske recalled that Miles "got off to an incredible start and it took a while before I could catch him."

**Nassau, December 1964**
Saunders races with Bob Grossman's Ferrari 250LM, left. In spite of a lack of international driving experience, Jack Saunders acquitted himself well. Penske begins to pull away from Miles' failing Cobra, below. Both the short-lived aluminum engine and leaf-spring suspension were about to give up the ghost, leaving Miles with a long walk back to the pits.

**Nassau, December 1964**
John Mecom watches the progress of his cars, above left. Jack Saunders, above, was never able to shake the Ford GT40s of Phil Hill (91) and Bruce McLaren (97) until they finally broke. Saunders retired on the eighteenth lap of the 23 lap race. Roger Penske drives through the pits to the applause of various crews, left, after taking the checkered flag in the Nassau Tourist Trophy race. The race was stopped because of rain and darkness.

130

**Nassau, December 1964**
Roger Penske and Jim Hall pick up the Nassau Tourist Trophy, far left. It was to be the first of three major victories for Penske, as he won both the Governor's Cup and Nassau Trophy races in addition to the Tourist Trophy. Penske's hat trick was a feat never before or since accomplished at Nassau. He announced his retirement from driving after the close of the 1964 Nassau Speed Week. George Wintersteen, left, would drive his first race in the Grand Sport at Nassau in 1964 in the 005 car, which he had purchased from Roger Penske.

**Nassau, December 1964**
The start of the Nassau Governor's Cup race. The two Grand Sports can be seen about one-third of the way back with a Sting Ray convertible between them.

**Nassau, December 1964**
At some point during the week between the Tourist Trophy and the Governor's Cup races, the Hall/Penske 005 Grand Sport was sold to George Wintersteen. Now sporting Wintersteen's well-known number 12, right, the car was run in the Governor's Cup race. Here, Wintersteen leads the Brabham BT8 of Hugh P. K. Dibley. Below, Jack Saunders laps the Alpine-Renault A110 of Ray Cuomo during the Governor's Cup race. Saunders again failed to finish, dropping out on the twenty-second lap of the 25 lap event. He was, however, classified as tenth overall.

**Nassau, December 1964**
At the start of the Nassau Trophy race,
the Wintersteen car is still on the line
as Foyt's Chrysler-powered Mecom
Hussein (1), Hudson (94), Penske's
Chaparral (6), Sharp's sideways
Chaparral (66) and Johnson's Cobra
(92) are on their way. Wintersteen
finished twenty-third overall although
he was not running at the finish.

**Nassau, December 1964**
The Wintersteen 005 Grand Sport limps through its last race after a shunt removed most of its front-end bodywork. The radiator and chassis are easily studied; note the branch hanging from the base of the radiator.
*Alice Bixler/Road & Track*

*Chapter 5*

# The beginning of the end, 1965

The 1965 running of the Sebring twelve-hour race marked an important change in American long-distance racing. For the first time, Ferrari was not the favored marque. "On Saturday at the sun-baked airfield outside this little town," said a particularly florid report in the *The Tampa Times*, "Ferrari begins its last stand against a corporate American onslaught. For the first time in 10 years, the red cars cannot be favored to win Sebring." That year's favorite, stated the anonymous UPI reporter, was Ford: "There is a saying in racing that nothing can beat cubic inches. This is not wholly accurate, for money is what nothing can beat. And the world of motor racing has never seen the kind of money the Ford Motor Co. is pouring into the sport." As for GM, the report noted that the automotive giant "washes its hands of a car after it is sold and refuses to have anything to do with it. Cars cannot hope to win in international endurance racing without the manufacturer's support." And that just about said it all.

In this environment, the Grand Sports really had no place to go. Without factory parts and engineering support, their competitiveness was ebbing. Furthermore, by the end of 1964, the sophistication of the Grand Sports' competitors in the prototype and sports-racing categories left the Corvettes little hope of shining in their front-engine configuration. How could they be expected to compete with the new Chaparrals, McLarens, Ferrari 330P2s or the all-new Lola T70? The answer was that they could not. Nonetheless, two stalwart owners laid plans to tackle Sebring in 1965.

## Assault on Sebring

After Nassau, George Wintersteen's ex-Hall/Penske 005 car was returned to the Penske/Wintersteen shop in Newtown Square, Pennsylvania, where it was prepared for Sebring by mechanic Bill Scott. As Scott remembered, "I ended up building an engine, it was a 364 ci engine, not a 377 ci as many people believe." Replacement bodywork was also required, and a stock Sting Ray front end was obtained from nearby Nickey Chevrolet and grafted onto the front of the Grand Sport.

Backed by substantial resources, Wintersteen was running essentially as a privateer, which gave him total liberty with his otherwise restricted Chevrolet prototype. At Sebring one night after the sun had set on a practice session, he decided to drive the car back to his off-airfield garage rather than trailering it. "I was having electrical problems with the car that night—we had to twist two wires together to keep it going—the ignition switch was disabled. I actually passed some guy on the outside of a curve on a public road. I was

spotted by a police car, who wanted to pull me over. I led the cops on a merry chase to the garage, where they put me against the car, frisked me and gave me a stern reprimand. The funniest thing was their effort to describe what I had been driving."

The second Sebring entry was the 003 Grand Sport, which John Mecom had sold to nineteen-year-old Alan Sevadjian of Arlington, Texas, for $7,500 in January 1965. Too young to race himself in the SCCA, Sevadjian's car would be piloted by his father, Ed.

According to Delmo Johnson, the Sevadjian car was to be prepared for Sebring at Johnson's Dallas Chevrolet dealership. About the time the car was to leave for Florida, Johnson received some interesting news: "One morning I received a call from Zora, and he said, 'Delmo, I'm sending you a special engine to put in the Grand Sport. It's race prepared and ready to go.' I said, 'That's great, when do I look for the box?' Zora said, 'No box. It will be coming to you from the St. Louis production line in a stock Corvette.'"

Johnson insisted that this engine was a 454 ci iron-block motor, although contemporary racing records list its displacement as 6780 cc, which is closer to 427 ci than 454. Whatever its actual displacement, it was clearly a special engine, for Johnson recalled that its serial number was stamped as XXXX1.

"It was a real prototype," said Johnson. "Zora had told us to just drop the engine in, but we decided to pull the oil pan anyway. Much to our surprise we found that someone had dropped a handful of cotter keys into the crankcase. Needless to say, we wouldn't have run very far in practice, and with no spare parts available, we would have really been hurting. We found out later that there had been some union problems at the St. Louis plant, but fortunately we had checked the engine and there was no damage."

The 003 Grand Sport's larger engine meant that the hood had to be modified once again. This time, two large holes—covered with the racing equivalent of chicken wire—were cut into the raised portion of the hood between the lateral vents that had previously been added to make room for the Weber carb setup.

The Sevadjian car would be driven by Johnson, Dave Morgan and the elder Sevadjian. Despite the special treatment from Arkus-Duntov in the engine department, however, the lack of a trained crew and spare parts was telling. During practice laps, Johnson recalled that Morgan let the car slip away from him, slapping its tail into a telephone pole. The resourceful Johnson simply taped up the damaged panels and then painted over the tape. But the accident also punched a hole in the gas tank and caused the plexiglass rear window to pop out. "We had problems with the gas tank," continued

**Sebring, March 1965**
The Johnson/Morgan Grand Sport in the pits during practice. The top of the hood has been cut away to provide more air for the iron big-block engine.

Johnson, "which was fiberglass. We repaired it, but wanted to run hard in practice and make sure it was fixed before we replaced the rear window and all of the rest of the parts."

But adequate preparation—or the lack of it—was overshadowed by the ominous weather forecasts. "All anybody talked about the night before the race," wrote Steve Smith in *Car and Driver*. "There were some pretty wild rumors. Hurricane. Tornado. Hail. Going down to 25 [degrees]." Despite the pessimistic predictions, however, the weather for the opening hours of the race was muggy and hot: 94 degrees Fahrenheit.

As soon as Florida Governor Ferris Bryant dropped the green flag at 10:00 am, Johnson was across the track and off to a fast start before a record crowd. So fast, in fact, that he threatened to get sideways as the Grand Sport's chassis struggled to cope with the big-block's awesome power. Like other Grand Sport drivers before and after, Johnson recalled nothing so much about the car as its tremendous acceleration and poor handling: "It was an ill-handling piece of junk that would go extremely fast in one direction only. About halfway down the [Warehouse] straight, I was out of control. The front end would come right off the ground, and you would lose steering. And at the end of the turn, it might or might not stop. Coming out of a corner, if I got on the power a little wrong, the more out of control it got."

## Heat and flood

Both teams did their best to cope with the heat. The Sevadjian/Johnson/Morgan team adjusted in mid-race by taping a tube to the right side of the car and into the passenger window that in the end directed more hot air into the cockpit. Wintersteen and co-driver Peter Goetz were less fortunate. After taking the 005 car over from Wintersteen on the eighteenth lap, Goetz eventually fell victim to the extraordinary temperatures. "It was hotter than hell," recalled Wintersteen. "Goetz succumbed to heat and just couldn't go on and [Milton] Diehl took over as an emergency addition."

---

**"It was an ill-handling piece of junk that would go extremely fast in one direction only."**
*Driver Delmo Johnson*

---

Racing against the Chaparrals, Ferrari 275Ps and Ford GT40s was bad enough, but nothing compared to the rain. At 5:30 pm, after 7½ hours of racing, the skies opened up and unleashed a deluge. On the track, cars that had been traveling 165 mph were suddenly humbled by zero visibility and water over a foot deep. Wrote Smith: "Phil Hill, driving a Cobra Daytona coupe after his (and Richie Ginther's) Ford GT went out with suspension mount fatigue, was up to his waist in water. 'Like it was being pumped in,' he said. Three times in one lap he stopped and opened the door to let the sloshing water out. Then, picking up speed again, he saw a turn loom out of the gray wall of water. Hill cranked the wheel violently and discovered he had turned into a parking lot." But it wasn't just the cars on the ground that had cause for worry: The Goodyear blimp, wrote race organizer Alec Ulmann, "stood vertically with its tail pointing to the sky, while the nose attached to the tethering mast was jerking to free itself."

Down on the ground, the Wintersteen team was faring well. At 11:00 am, they were in tenth position, trailing Ed Hugus' Ferrari 275P. Although they never again climbed into the top ten, the car managed to stay together. Recalled owner Wintersteen: "How can I forget the year of the great flood? I would have water inside the car, and when I took my foot off the clutch, there would be a great splash. It was embarrassing to have the Sprites go by you in the straightaway. In spite of that, we had a reasonably troublefree race and we never stopped. The biggest problem we faced was that we were placed in the Prototype class with the Ford GT40s, so we had little chance of a class win."

At the end of the 1,019.2 mile event, Wintersteen and Diehl finished a respectable fourteenth overall—second in class—which, judged Wintersteen, wasn't too bad under the circumstances. After the race, mechanic Bill Scott tore down the engine and found that the car had ingested a fair amount of water. "In fact," Wintersteen recalled, "two of the connecting rods had a visible bend in them."

The Sevadjian/Johnson/Morgan car had its share of problems, including a faulty throttle linkage. At one point, recalled Johnson, a bolt retaining the linkage inside the cockpit loosened, rendering the pedal useless. Johnson failed to give up, however, and simply stood up on the sill panel, opened up the hood, and coaxed the car back into the pits. In spite of its musclebound powerplant, however, it finished thirty-sixth overall, nearly sixty laps behind the winning Hall/Sharp Chaparral and more than thirty laps behind Wintersteen's Grand Sport.

## Last days of the coupes

Johnson retired from racing after that year's Sebring—almost. Two weeks later, he went to Green Valley to see Ed Sevadjian race his son's Grand Sport 003 in an SCCA event. Johnson had gone to the race as a spectator, but somehow managed to talk Sevadjian into letting him drive the last race. Although the jig was up after the first lap as the officials caught wind of the switch, Johnson stuck with it, eventually lapping the Shelby Mustang GT350 that had beat Sevadjian in an earlier race. "I didn't go out there to lose," recalled Johnson.

While George Wintersteen and Alan Sevadjian took part in the last acts of the Grand Sport drama, the 004 coupe, which Johnson had previously sold to Dave Greenblatt, was doing its best in Canadian events, where it was sponsored by Duval Chevrolet of Montreal and driven by Jacques Coutures. As with the Johnson car, a big-block was fitted that, according to contemporary photos, appears to have been fitted with a high-rise, cross-ram manifold topped by dual downdraft four-barrel carbs.

Despite its competitive shortcomings, Coutures fared well with the Grand Sport. In the Players Quebec Race held at the Circuit Mt. Tremblant in St. Jovite, Coutures started twenty-sixth in a field of twenty-seven and finished eighth overall against a vastly superior field. At the Canadian Grand Prix for Sports Cars at Mosport in

September 1965, Coutures started fourteenth out of twenty-nine. Running among Jim Hall in a Chaparral 2C and Hugh P. K. Dibley's Lola T70, the Grand Sport ran well until an oil leak forced it to retire.

The 004 coupe was subsequently returned to the United States when it was acquired by Jim White Chevrolet. Despite its antiquity, White chose to campaign it in the 1967 Daytona twenty-four-hour race, with drivers Tony Denman and B. Brown. Given that the Grand Sports could barely survive Sebring, however, a good show-ing at Daytona was even less likely. Moreover, it was racing against such state-of-the-art mid-engine cars as the Ferrari 330P4 and the Ford GT40 Mk IIB. White's car lasted seventy-two laps before retir-ing with unknown problems.

The 1967 Daytona assault marked the Grand Sports' final attempt at a big win, a disappointing and inconclusive finish to a project that had held so much promise.

**Green Valley, Texas, February 1965**
After officially retiring at Sebring in 1964, Delmo Johnson briefly returned to racing at this SCCA regional race to drive Alan Sevadjian's ex-Mecom Grand Sport 003. *Bill Neale*

**Sebring, March 1965**
If the Johnson/Morgan 004 Grand Sport looks as if it is running without a rear window, you're right. The window saw damage when Morgan went off course during practice.

**Sebring, March 1965**
The left front brakes of the 004 Grand Sport, with Girling calipers and vented discs. Note air duct in the lower left corner of the wheelhouse.

**Sebring, March 1965**
Starting in twentieth position, Delmo Johnson gets sideways off the line well ahead of the field at the beginning of the 12 hour race. Behind him is an Iso-Bizzarini Grifo A3 Corsa running in the prototype class as well. At the start of the lineup are two Chaparrals, the drivers still buckling their seatbelts.

**Sebring, March 1965**

As the rest of the field comes alive, Johnson is still sideways as he accelerates hard down the pit straight. "The car had so much power," said Johnson, "I didn't know how I was going to straighten it out before the first corner." Behind him is the Iso Grifo (8) with its partner coming off the line as well (9). The Chaparral drivers are still playing with their seatbelts while one of the first Lola T70s (22) blasts away. The Cobra Daytona coupes (12 and 15) are also starting off behind a Ferrari 275P (32). Down the line, two Alfa Romeo TZ 1s are charging off.

**Sebring, March 1965**
The race is on! George Wintersteen's Grand Sport 003 is away in the middle of the pack as the two Chaparrals finally get in gear. The field included a Ford GT40 (11), Ferrari 250 GTO (35), several Porsches and Cobras, the two Alfas (55 and 56), a Jaguar E-Type, Austin-Healey, Volvo P1800, and several MGs and Triumphs.

**Sebring, March 1965**

In the early laps, both Grand Sports were among the front runners, left. The Johnson/Payne Cobra Daytona coupe leads Delmo Johnson, David Piper's Ferrari 250LM and others. At top, the Piper/Maggs Ferrari 250LM leads the Wintersteen Grand Sport (2), the Grossman/Hudson/Hayes Ferrari 330P (26), the Johnson Grand Sport and the Decker/Koveleski Cooper-Ford (21). The Johnson/Morgan Grand Sport, above, laps the Abarth-Simca 2000 of Swanson/Ennis/Layman.

**Sebring, March 1965**
The Wintersteen/Goetz/Diehl Grand Sport leads a Ferrari 250LM through one of Sebring's turns, right. This car was in tenth place at the end of the first hour, the highest placing of any Grand Sport during the 1965 Sebring Race. The two Grand Sports, below, apply power out of a corner at the same moment, side-by-side, both in controlled slides.

**Sebring, March 1965**
The Johnson/Morgan Grand Sport in
the pits. The car is undergoing a tire
change and an engine check. Dave
Morgan, at left in helmet, awaits his
turn at the wheel.

145

**Sebring, March 1965**
Through the Webster Turns, right, the Wintersteen/Goetz car chases the Ferrari 275P of Hugus/O'Brien. The Johnson/Morgan car is pursued through the Webster Turns by the Ferrari 330P of Fulp/Kolb/McCluskey, below. Note the air ducts under the headlight covers to cool the brakes and the revival of the hood air dam, first used in the early races of 1963.

**Sebring, March 1965**
The Wintersteen/Goetz/Diehl Grand Sport leads the Johnson/Payne Cobra Daytona coupe down the long back straight past a large assortment of airplanes, top. Note the plane at the upper left, coming in over the cars, for a landing. The Johnson/Morgan Grand Sport at speed, above. Note the rubber ventilating hose in the right window, which was this team's way of coping with the terrible heat and humidity during this event. Despite the high speeds, this feeble attempt at air conditioning was not terribly successful.

**Sebring, March 1965**
The Wintersteen/Goetz/Diehl car on the straight with the Johnson/Payne Cobra Daytona coupe and the Grossman/Hudson Ferrari 330P, right. Grand Sport 004 ran a reasonably troublefree race and finished fourteenth overall, second in class. This was the highest finish any Grand Sport would ever have at Sebring. The Johnson/Morgan car in for one of its many pit stops, below. Note that all of the hood vents have been taped up in preparation for the coming rain.

**Sebring, March 1965**
The worst rainstorm to ever hit
Sebring has come and gone, and the
Johnson/Morgan Grand Sport races
across the dark, wet course.

149

**Sebring, March 1965**
The Johnson/Morgan car makes its
final night pit stop. This car finished
thirty-sixth overall in spite of suffering
a multitude of problems, including a
blown transmission and spark plug
trouble.

**St. Jovite, Canada, September 1965**
Little is known of the 005 Grand Sport after it was sold by Johnson to Canadian Dave Greenblatt in late 1965, left. Campaigned to some extent in Canadian events, it was sponsored by Duval Chevrolet in Montreal and driven by Canadian driver Jacques Coutures. The car, shown here during practice for the Player's Quebec Race in September 1965, is believed to have been powered by a 427 Chevrolet engine with a high-rise, cross-ram manifold and dual four-barrel carbs. The Duval Grand Sport at speed during the Player's Quebec Race held at Circuit Mt. Tremblant in St. Jovite, Canada, below. Coutures started twenty-sixth in a field of 27 and finished eighth overall against vastly superior competition. Note the world's ugliest hood.

**Mosport, September 1965**

The Duval 005 car, right, was entered in the Canadian Grand Prix for Sports Cars at Mosport, also in September 1965. The Grand Sport is lined up for practice alongside John Surtees in his Lola T70. Surtees looks somewhat dubious about the Grand Sport's hood. On race day, below, the Grand Sport started in fourteenth position in a 29 car field. Here, the car is running fifth in a group of cars headed by Lothar Motschenbacker in a Cooper-Ford (20) and Jim Hall in his Chaparral 2C (66).

**Daytona, February 1967**
Grand Sport coupe 004 showed up at the Daytona 24 hour race in February 1967, left. The coupe was bought from Dave Greenblatt in Canada by Jim White Chevrolet. This well-raced car was to be driven by the team of Tony Denman and B. Brown. The car is undergoing preparation for the race in the team garage. Note that the hood has been altered yet again with a hole finally cut through the top for the two carbs to breathe. The 427 powered car sits in the pits prior to the start of the race, below. Note the extra driving lights protected by wire cages, the dash-mounted tach and the ventilation scoop on the roof. The exhaust pipe has also grown in size.

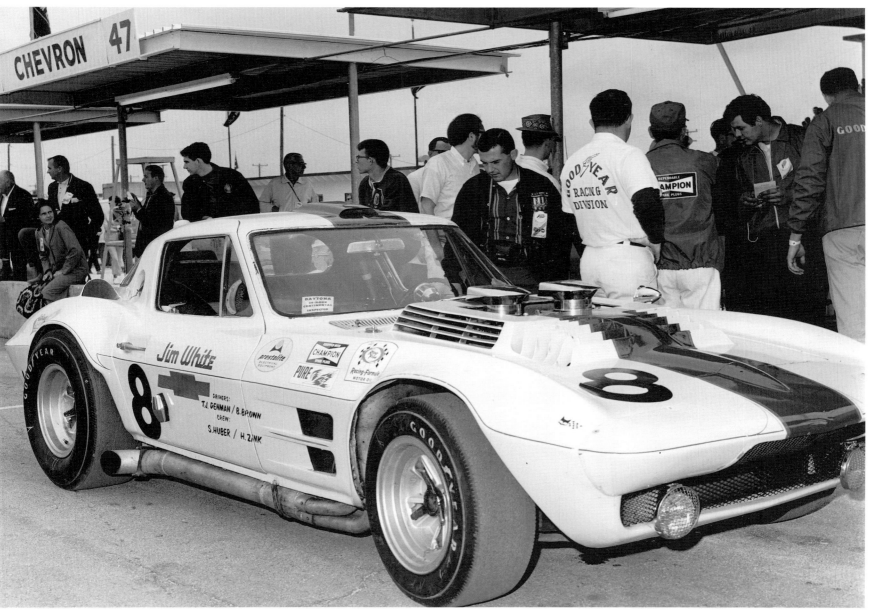

**Daytona, February 1967**
The 004 car, with Tony Denman at the wheel, left, is seen on the famous high banks of the Daytona Speedway. The car was never anywhere close to being a front runner. Exotic machines like the Ferrari 330P4 and the Ford GT40 Mk IIB made running the Grand Sport a rather hopeless situation. The 004 Grand Sport during one of its many pit stops, right. The car lasted 72 laps before retiring with unknown problems.

It looked and sounded like a Grand Sport. It was entered at the Road America 500 in 1965, 1966 and 1967 as a Corvette Grand Sport, but in fact it was not a Grand Sport. Driven by the team of Martin/Schoenfeld, below, the car finished the race in the top 15 all three years. Little is known on how the car came to be, but by all the records in the author's possession, there is no question that this was not a true Grand Sport.

# Chapter 6

# The roadsters' last gasp

If the Grand Sports were dinosaurs at Sebring in 1965, then they were fossils the following year, when Lorenzo Bandini and his lilliputian two-liter Ferrari Dino 206S would—albeit briefly—tear away from a field of seven-liter GT40s. Nonetheless, Roger Penske believed that the Grand Sports might still be competitive, and in early 1966 arranged to buy the last two remaining cars—001 and 002—from Chevrolet, keeping 001 for himself and selling sibling 002 to friend George Wintersteen. Both owners had their work cut out for them.

Unlike the Grand Sport coupes, the 001 and 002 cars carried roadster bodies in order to maximize their top speed for planned attacks on the 1964 Daytona 2,000 kilometer Continental and Sebring twelve-hour races, with the possibility of Le Mans later that year. Just how these two chassis came to be topless remains unclear. Some say that the cars were cut down into roadster form, while others maintain they were bare chassis until receiving their roadster bodies. Whatever their provenance, it is fairly certain that the 001 Grand Sport was originally bodied as a coupe, as it was probably the car tested at Sebring in December 1962. Much less is known about the second roadster, 002, which was not released by Chevrolet until its sale to Penske, suggesting that it may have been a roadster from the start. Nonetheless, contemporary Chevrolet photos of the first two cars under construction show both with coupe bodies, which would again suggest that the roadster configuration was a later update. In any event, the Grand Sport's simplified skin would have made it relatively easy to modify its silhouette without creating an entirely new body.

But it was all for naught. Arkus-Duntov's ambitious plans for the 1964 season collapsed when GM pulled the plug on the Grand Sport effort after its announcement that the corporation was in no way associated with John Mecom and disbanded the program. While the three coupes were sold off in early 1964, the roadsters—according to some insiders—were scheduled to be destroyed, the fate of many a redundant prototype or dream car. Yet somehow they survived, probably because knowledge of their existence was limited to the few insiders who knew or cared what they were or where they were stored.

And that's where they stayed, at least until the spring of 1965, when one of the roadsters showed up at a Notre Dame University auto show on temporary loan from Chevrolet thanks to a student's benevolent GM executive father. About the only notice it received was a brief mention in *Car Life*, which incorrectly stated that it was constructed with an aluminum chassis. Just where this exotic proto-type might be raced *Car Life* didn't mention, but its wistful conclusion might well have been based on inside knowledge: "Just think," mused the anonymous author, "what a Grand Sport equipped with one of Chevrolet's new 427 NASCAR engines . . . would do."

## Penske and Grand Sport . . . again

Strangely enough, Roger Penske's thinking ran along similar lines. At the time, Chevrolet's 427 ci Mark II Daytona Mystery Motor had matured into the tamer—albeit plenty powerful—Mark IV 396 ci production engine, output ranging from 325 hp in the Impala to 425 hp in the Corvette. Its availability as a $300 option on the latter—where it undercut the L84 fuel-injected 327 ci by over $200—was not to Arkus-Duntov's liking as he preferred to refine the fuel-injected small-block as a route to more power. Nonetheless, Penske was confident that a marriage between the Mark IV big-block and the Grand Sport chassis might be just the thing to hold back the seven-liter Cobras and GT40s. Not long after his November 1964 Nassau hat trick, he told *Corvette News:* "I feel that with Chevrolet's new 396 engine and our experience running the Lightweight and other cars the last five years, I think we can continue to be a thorn in the side of the factory teams."

But before Penske could put his plan into action, he had bigger things to worry about. After retiring from racing following his Nassau honors, he focused his energies on the burgeoning Chevrolet dealership he had taken over from George McKean. Once that was off the ground, he would be in the position to start a team of his own, and that required sponsors. Given his record and reputation, however, that would hardly be difficult, and help soon issued forth from Sun Oil Marketing Vice President Elmer Bradley, who had purchased a Corvette at Penske's dealership. Starting in 1966, Sunoco actively supported Penske's Corvette efforts, in addition to providing hands-on assistance in the form of mechanic and expert machinist Bill Scott (who had been informally associated with Penske since the Zerex Special days) and technical advisor Bill Preston.

The first member of Penske's fledgling equipe would be a production-based 1966 Corvette coupe, equipped, not surprisingly, with the top Corvette engine, the dimensions of which had grown from 396 ci in 1965 to 427 ci once GM repealed its internal 400 ci engine limit. His choice to drive it was not one of the new matadors with whom he had teamed previously, but a less well-known driver from Los Angeles named Dick Guldstrand.

By the time Guldstrand was brought to Penske's attention by Arkus-Duntov and Chevrolet racing maven Joe Pike, he had won three consecutive regional SCCA championships in Baher Chevrolet-sponsored C-Production Sting Rays, successfully turning back the Cobras. "I could beat them every once in a while if they made a mistake," said Guldstrand of his favorite enemies. "I couldn't beat them one on one, but if somebody screwed up..." That meant some hard driving in a car that still wasn't the equal of its Shelby counterpart, earning Guldstrand no little notoriety for driving at the limit—and beyond. "My Corvette handled extremely well, but I had to drive my ass off, so I got upside down a lot," he said. "That's why I got a roller skate mounted on my roll bar. I either crashed or won, but I got a lot of attention nationally."

The production coupe that Penske and company would take to Daytona and Sebring was delivered right off the St. Louis line, at which point Guldstrand drove it to the Penske shop in Newtown Square, Pennsylvania. The car came with a few special options, of course, not all of which were available in the showroom. Its engine was a new 427, but equipped with aluminum heads—the predecessor of the 1967 L88 option. Since it was to be raced, it was devoid of any creature comforts, including a heater and radio, which meant that Guldstrand's trip north would be a cold, quiet one.

While the Sting Ray coupe was being prepared, Penske purchased the two Grand Sport roadsters and arranged for Guldstrand, Scott and Wintersteen mechanic Bill "Murph" Mayberry to pick up his 001 car in Warren and bring it back to Pennsylvania. Guldstrand was responsible for getting it ready for Sebring (only the production coupe would go to Daytona), which was something of a challenge considering that the car had been mothballed in 1964. "Since the car had sat untouched for two years," he said, "we tore it completely apart and started rebuilding from scratch."

According to Guldstrand, its engine was to be one of the 427 ci Daytona Mystery Motors, and it was sent to Traco Engineering in Culver City, California, to be race-prepared. "I supervised the engine preparation," recalled Guldstrand. "Since we were after durability rather than massive horsepower, we actually de-tuned the engine to about 500 bhp. I had a guy by the name of Jerry Stall build

**Sebring, March 1966**
Dick Thompson pulls away from the sprint start in the Grand Sport roadster 001. The Ford GT40 Mk IIs of Walt Hansgen (3) and eventual race winner Ken Miles (1) are just getting started.

157

the header system. We knew it was very easy to blow up that engine and that they had oiling problems in the past.

"We also had to modify the front springs to accept the extra weight of the 427 engine. There was no problem getting it in there—it went right in. My concern was redoing all the stuff that held it up—the front springs and shocks—to make sure that it would handle. Our biggest problem was that everything was so rushed that we had no development time on the car before we left for Sebring."

Yet even with the extra weight of the iron-block 427 up front, Guldstrand was worried about that traditional Grand Sport bugaboo, front-end lift. "With the power that we were going to get in the Lightweight, I was very concerned about understeer, and about the front end pulling up, which it did. So we added a spoiler under the nose to keep it down and lightened the frame." Guldstrand also installed the same air jack/oil/water system that Penske had used previously at Sebring to dramatically shorten pit stops, and removed the fairing on the rear deck that was mounted behind the driver's head.

### Last stand at Sebring

Penske's 001 roadster finally met the public at Sebring in late March 1966, with Dick Guldstrand and Dick Thompson sharing driving duties. There, it joined the production coupe (a class winner at Daytona), which would be driven by Wintersteen and Ben Moore. Nearly three years after its original completion, the front-engined Grand Sport was almost embarrassingly out of place in a prototype field composed of state-of-the-art Ford GT40s, Chaparrals, Ferrari Dinos and Porsche 904s. Nonetheless, said Guldstrand, the long-dormant roadster put on a good show: "For an old front-engined car, we sure made them know that we were there. The car was a dinosaur—it was the last of the front-engined cars. Everyone was into mid-engine cars by then, but we were proud of our effort."

As with the coupe, the Penske team experimented with aluminum heads for the roadster's 427 engine, which slightly reduced the weight on its front springs. Nevertheless, recalled Dick Thompson, they never made it to the actual race: "Jim Travers [of Traco Engineering] brought some aluminum heads to Sebring, but we had problems with them due to lack of development time, so we switched back to the iron heads." It hardly mattered, however, for the roadster's engine was plenty powerful. "They could out-brake us and out-corner us," said Guldstrand of the newer cars, "but on the straights, nothing at Sebring could stay with the roadster.

"We were housed back at the Webster garages, which meant that we could come out onto the Warehouse Straight without having to use the normal entrance for practice. So we'd pull out with the Fords and blow them off. Foyt couldn't believe it when we flew by his Mark II. He came up to me in the pits and said, 'What's in that damn dinosaur? It went by me like I was stopped.'"

The price for all that power was a prodigious tendency for the car to behave like a dragster—in any gear. "You had to be very careful off the line with that car," said Guldstrand. "You had to feather the throttle, because if you stood on the gas, you could pull the goddamn tires off the ground."

Power alone would not decide the roadster's destiny. After making a strong start, Thompson settled at thirteenth position by the end of the first hour, turning in the car's top lap time of 3:10.0 just after 11:00 am. By the end of the third hour, the car had fallen to sixteenth position after climbing as high as twelfth.

---

**"As far as I'm concerned, if any driver ever says he had complete control of that car, he's lying to you."**
*Driver Delmo Johnson*

---

At 1:44 pm, however, while going under the Dunlop Bridge, Thompson was forced off the road at high speed while passing a Morgan. Recalled Sunoco's Bill Preston: "Thompson hit a Morgan and went off the course between a telephone pole and its supporting guy wire. There were houses along that section of the track in those days, and he went through a backyard and across a driveway that was a good foot below the lawn. Somewhere along in there, the car bent its tubular frame." Added Thompson, "I remember taking down a clothesline at one point. But the real problem was the damage to the coil springs in front. After getting back on the course, the car became very difficult to handle." Unbeknownst to Thompson at the time, the exhaust system had been damaged during his off-course excursion, which in turn punctured the oil pan.

In the meantime, Guldstrand was waiting to get in the car when Penske approached him: "Roger came over and said, 'Goldie, I think we got a problem.'" When Thompson eventually limped back into the pits with no oil pressure, it was clearly terminal. Sunoco had dyed the engine oil green and the transmission and rear axle oil red to simplify troubleshooting. When the hood was opened, recalled Preston, the engine "had green oil all over it. But it also had been cranked over at an angle." And with that, the Thompson/Guldstrand 001 car was out of the race after completing just sixty-five laps.

Following the Sebring shortfall, the 001 roadster was turned over briefly to John Mecom and later sold to Jerry Hanna of Pasadena, Texas, who continued to campaign it in various SCCA events. Somewhere along the way it was slightly modified, with 1966 Corvette-style vertical fender vents in place of the horizontal versions used originally; bolt-on rear wheels replaced the original Halibrand knock-offs.

### The Wintersteen roadster

As for the 002 Grand Sport, it was shortly after Sebring that Wintersteen traveled west to retrieve it from Chevrolet. "Roger and I had become good friends at the time," Wintersteen recalled. "He said, 'There's another one of these cars at GM.' Racing was getting expensive, and I was looking for a way to stay in it, so I bought the car—chassis 002—from Roger and picked it up after Sebring." He was met in Warren by Arkus-Duntov, who delighted in showing off his collection of custom-made high-performance vehicles. "There were all sorts of exotic things there," said Wintersteen. "Duntov was like a kid in a toy shop, bubbling with enthusiasm, lifting up a tarp here, a tarp there."

As with Penske's roadster, the Wintersteen car went back to the shop in Newtown Square, where it, too, received a more muscular powerplant. "We were running a blueprinted 427 with a big Holley carb in the roadster," recalled Wintersteen. "It had lots of power but not like the one that Penske ran at Sebring [001]. That car had . . . unbelievable horsepower. It was really something to see." In order to fit the larger engine in the 002 chassis, Wintersteen recalled, a notch had to be removed from the Grand Sport's front crossmember. To solve the nagging knock-off wheel problem, Wintersteen fitted bolt-on American Racing magnesium alloys front and rear. And, like Penske, he removed the fairing behind the driver's head.

Wintersteen was planning to campaign his car in the United States Road Racing Championship, the SCCA's series for professional drivers; the car would be something of an antique. "I knew it was obsolete in the pro ranks when I bought it. The Lolas and McLarens were starting to become quite reliable. But for that year, it was an economical way to go racing," Wintersteen remembered.

Among its earliest trials was the Bridgehampton USRRC in May 1966. Although outclassed by the Lolas and McLarens, car and driver gave a good account of themselves, finishing seventeenth overall and eighth in the over-two-liter class.

---

"It was so light in the front end that when you really stood on the gas, the front end would come off the ground like a dragster."
*Driver Roger Penske*

---

At Watkins Glen in June, Wintersteen's finishing position is not known, but he does remember a run-in with Charlie Parsons' McLaren. "Coming over the hill at the Glen, I kept feeling a bump as I crested the hill. I thought it was a rock on the course, but it was Parsons trying to move me over. I had the line through the corner and I intended to move over and let him pass on the straight, but he was in a hurry and tried to pass me on the inside of the corner. The next thing I knew, Parsons was off in the weeds amid great clouds of dust."

Wintersteen also has distinct memories about the Grand Sport's performance and handling characteristics, particularly its acceleration: "It was quick on the straights, but its aerodynamics were terrible. At Watkins Glen and some of the quick tracks, the front end was getting right up there . . . It would go down the straights looking like a speedboat." Nonetheless, said Wintersteen, it was not a difficult car to drive. "It had very good brakes and a locked rear end—we just welded the spiders together. Although it had a lot of power, it was light in the rear end. You wound up just steering with the throttle."

Needless to say, the Grand Sport roadsters, with bodywork that was even more exotic than that of the coupes, attracted much attention. Wintersteen recalled an incident that took place on the Long Island Expressway one evening while he and Mayberry were towing their Grand Sport on an open trailer to Bridgehampton. "Murph was driving the truck; all of a sudden, he swerved to avoid a series of collisions that were taking place ahead of us. Fortunately, Murph was smart enough to dive to the right. Just as we got everything stabilized, we heard a great crash as the driver of the car that had been following us—whose attention was on the Grand Sport and not on the traffic—crashed into the car in front of him."

Wintersteen's last race with the 002 roadster was the Players 200 at Mosport in June 1966, where he finished ninth overall. He later sold the car to Georgian John Thorne for $6,700, thinking—like Delmo Johnson—that he had gotten the better part of the deal. Today he feels differently: "I wish to hell I still had the Grand Sport."

## The orphan

And that pretty much was that, as far as the roadsters were concerned. Thereafter, only sporadic and unsuccessful attempts would be made to race them. As they became increasingly uncompetitive—and increasingly difficult to repair—they soon degraded from competitors into curiosities, treasured not as glorious chariots that had burnished the Chevrolet name to a bright shine, but banished as expensive, embarrassing failures best forgotten.

But imagine what might have been, had Chevrolet focused its tremendous engineering resources on the development of a lightweight, sophisticated dual-purpose GT that would finally win for America the European laurels it had so long been denied—with a purely American car and not a hybrid. "If only they'd done the job right to begin with," mused Corvette veteran Guldstrand. "They were supposed to turn back the Cobras, and that's exactly what they would have done if they could have been homologated. As it was, they raced in a class for which they weren't prepared, and that was the sad part.

"Chevrolet did have a better motor, and their technology was better—with a good suspension it would have been a hell of a show. If it had clicked—if they had started winning races and it had caught on . . . Of course they would have sold special cars just like they did in the solid axle days when you could buy a race car with ducting in the quarter panels, vented brakes and a big gas tank—everything that you needed to go racing.

"But the Grand Sport was really dead the day it was born, and who wants to play with something that was very embarrassing, something that was costing a lot of people a lot of humiliation and pride? When Foyt, Penske and the others drove them at Nassau, they won races. But that was the end. Once Chevrolet found out about what was really going on, they destroyed all the tooling and orphaned the five cars.

"What's sad about General Motors," he concluded, "is that they have no feeling whatsoever for cars of this kind. They should have one of everything that they've ever built. But they don't, and that's awful."

One of the Grand Sport roadsters—chassis number 001 or 002—while still at the Chevrolet factory, above. The photograph was taken on April 2, 1964, soon after the two cars were completed. The Grand Sport roadster from the back, right. Note that all the modifications that were made to the three coupes during their racing careers also found their way onto the roadster bodywork; someone at Chevrolet was keeping close tabs. The fairing behind the driver's head was later removed from both cars for competition work. *Road & Track*

In the spring of 1965, one of the roadsters turned up at a Notre Dame car show, above left, courtesy of a GM executive whose son was attending the University. Note the clear plexiglass headlamp covers, interesting hood fastener and the odd filler cap on the driver-side fender. The engine of the roadster on show at Notre Dame in 1965, above. The race lessons have been well-learned. The cross-ram manifolds and the monster Weber DCOE carbs look as if they are straight off of the Mecom Nassau car; the chromed valve covers are a bit more showy. *Road & Track*

### Sebring, March 1966

Night work on Grand Sport roadster 001 in the hangars used as garages at Sebring, left. Roger Penske is adjusting something on the inside of the right door while Bill Mayberry works on the engine. Taping the left front headlight is Norman Ahn, now vice president of the Penske Corporation. Plainly visible is the Holley four-barrel carburetor on top of the 427 ci engine, and the connections for the air jacks and the oil and water fittings. The Penske team had added a full windshield to the roadster, bolting on molding to the abbreviated pillars.

**Sebring, March 1966**

Based on the experience of previous Grand Sports, holes were drilled on the rear panel of the Penske roadster to help cool the brakes and rear axle, right. The quick-fill gas cap is also visible here, as is the enclosed roll bar. A new hood scoop has been fitted to make way for the carbs. Note the dash-mounted rearview mirror and the Prova Italianesque plate. The Grand Sport roadster draws spectators as it is presented for inspection, below. Note the extra driving lights below the front grille.

For years, Dick Guldstrand was one of the West Coast's most successful Corvette drivers. He was signed by Penske as one of his original drivers and, because of his engineering background, was put in charge of preparing the Grand Sport roadster for the 1966 Sebring race. He co-drove the Grand Sport roadster with Dick Thompson.

**Sebring, March 1966**
Sebring version of the Le Mans start. Penske's Corvette coupe (9) is away from the line first, driven by George Wintersteen. Next off the mark is Dick Thompson in the Grand Sport roadster (10) and Pedro Rodriguez in the NART Ferrari 330P2/3 (26). Coming from behind are a TR4 Triumph (39) and the Andrey/Geki Autodelta Alfa Romeo TZ 2 (63).

**Sebring, March 1966**
Hot off the line, right, Rodriguez' 330P2/3 (26) and Lorenzo Bandini in the Ferrari Dino 206S (46) pull away from the Corvettes—momentarily. Seen through the heatwaves, below, Bandini (46), in his Dino, turns his head in time to watch the Grand Sport roadster closing on him. "Look at that thing honker down and hook up," said Dick Guldstrand. "God, what a start! You can see that goofy spoiler we made to try and keep the nose down, but it didn't help; the car had so much power that it was impossible to keep that nose down." Thompson blows by the Augie Pabst/Masten Gregory Ford GT40, far right. Said Guldstrand: "We had that thing working great, but the air would get underneath and start lifting the nose . . . The front wheels would come off the ground at 150 mph."

**Sebring, March 1966**
Guldstrand leads the Revson/Scott GT40 and the Andrey/Geki Alfa TZ 2 through the Webster Turns, top. The roadster slides out of The Hairpin, above, as a Shelby Mustang GT350 runs into the sand bank. Guldstrand: "That car had so much potential, it's too bad we didn't have it in 1964 when it was supposed to run."

**Sebring, March 1966**
Guldstrand, top, pulls out of the Webster Turns trailed by Ferrari's first 250 GTO chassis number 3223 GT.

Thompson on the Warehouse Straight, above. During the 3½ hours that it ran, the car was ranked as high as twelfth overall. Thompson recalled,

"It's too bad someone didn't take the time to develop that car because it has such tremendous potential. With an 1,800 pound car and a 427 ci

aluminum engine putting out 600 hp, it would have been quite something on a long, smooth course."

168

**Sebring, March 1966**
Dick Thompson in the Webster Turns leads the Bentley/Byrne/Lotta Cobra 427 and one of the Comstock Ford GT40s. Plainly visible on the Grand Sport is the spoiler under the front end and also the scoops for cooling the front brakes. At 1:34 pm, while passing under the Dunlop Bridge, Thompson was forced off the road at high speed by a Morgan. After the race, mechanic Bill Scott remembered that "when we got back to the shop, I had to get the car back in shape less the engine. It was then sold to John Mecom."

The 001 roadster, right, was subsequently sold to Jerry Hanna of Pasadena, Texas, who campaigned it in SCCA events. Note the 1966 style vertical fender vents, bolt-on rear wheels, small front air dam and rear deck lid spoiler. Color scheme was two-tone light and dark blue with an orange stripe. Note that the windshield has been cut back again.

**Bridgehampton, May 1966**
The Grand Sport 002 roadster was sold to George Wintersteen. According to Penske Vice President Norman Ahn, Wintersteen's car "was prepared in our shop by Bill Mayberry. In those days we all shared the same facility." One of its earliest outings took place at the Bridgehampton USRRC in May 1966. Although outclassed by the Lolas and McLarens, Wintersteen and the roadster gave a good account of themselves, finishing seventeenth overall and eighth in the over-two-liter class. The car was powered by a 427 ci iron-block engine, and retained its low-cut windshield.

**Cumberland, Maryland, May 1966**
The George Wintersteen crew at work on the 427 ci engine powering Grand Sport roadster 002 in preparation for the race, left. *Charles F. Sowers, Jr.*

**Watkins Glen, June 1966**
Wintersteen at speed, below. He started in twenty-sixth position and moved up well during an accident-marred race.

**Watkins Glen, June 1966**
Wintersteen and John Morton in a
Lotus-Porsche racing head-to-head
during the Watkins Glen USRRC, top.

George Wintersteen leads the Porsche
906 of Robert Treischmann
up the hill at Watkins Glen, above.
After Mark Donohue crashed his Lola

T70, Wintersteen stopped his car and
pulled Donohue from the burning
wreck. Wintersteen does not
remember the Donohue incident, but

does remember feeling Charlie
Parson's McLaren bump him and
then go off course.

**Mosport, June 1966**
The Grand Sport 002 roadster takes the wide line through a turn during the Players 200 at Mosport, Canada.

## Mosport, June 1966

Starting twenty-third, Wintersteen began to move up and ran with this pack for some time, above. "I could move up on the custom-built rear-engine cars, but I had no chance against the factory-built cars." The intent George Wintersteen at work in the cockpit of his roadster, right. Note the sculpted fairing that covers the roll bar. "Murph" is the nickname of Bill Mayberry, Wintersteen's mechanic. "If I had this car in 1965 when the English and Anglo-American cars were still rather crude," said Wintersteen, "I'd have done much better with it. Unfortunately for me, by 1966 the Lolas and McLarens were becoming much more refined and the only way I could beat them was on consistency."

## Mosport, June 1966

Dueling for eighth place with a Porsche 906, left, George Wintersteen here leads the Chaparral-like Chinook driven by George Fejer. Wintersteen finished ninth overall, which was a good showing considering the quality of the competition. McLaren cars took the first three positions, with Bruce McLaren taking the win. A good dice, below, between Bob Montana's McKee and the Wintersteen roadster; the promising McKee car was a DNF. Wintersteen recalled that his roadster was "a very light car with lots of power and fantastic brakes. There were very few cars who could pass me on the straight, but in the corners the English cars really prevailed. It was a very easy car for me to drive, although I'm glad I never had to drive it in the rain; that would have been a handful. The tight turns were pretty difficult in that car due to the locked rear end, but it was one of the most fun cars I ever drove."

# Index